OVERHEAD VISUALS COPYMASTERS

Including:
- **POUR COMMUNIQUER** *Supplementary Situational Overhead Visuals*
- **SUGGESTED EXPANSION ACTIVITIES**

DISCOVERING FRENCH

BLANC

Jean-Paul Valette

Rebecca M. Valette

The **Discovering French** Overhead Visuals contain original drawings and selected maps, photos, and illustrations from the Student Text. They may be used for a wide range of creative classroom activities, including:

- Listening comprehension practice
- TPR activities
- Speaking activities
- Building geography awareness
- Encouraging guided practice
- Providing opportunity for self-expression

D.C. Heath and Company
A Division of Houghton Mifflin Company

D.C. Heath and Company
A Division of Houghton Mifflin Company

Copyright © 1997 by D.C. Heath and Company, a Division of Houghton Mifflin Company

Permission to reproduce these pages for classroom use is granted to users of ***Discovering French–Blanc.***

Published simultaneously in Canada
Printed in the United States of America
International Standard Book Number: 0–669–43512-0

1 2 3 4 5 6 7 8 9 10 –BA– 01 00 99 98 97 96

Contents

Blanc Overhead Visuals

Overhead Visuals are correlated by page number to the *Discovering French–Blanc Extended Teacher's Edition.** Situational Visuals can be used at the end of each unit to integrate and recycle functions, vocabulary, or themes.

*The Overhead Visuals may also be used at many other points in the Program.

Contents—Overhead Visuals *(continued)*

Contents—Overhead Visuals (continued)

Contents—Overhead Visuals *(continued)*

DISCOVERING FRENCH

BLANC

POUR COMMUNIQUER:

SUPPLEMENTARY SITUATIONAL OVERHEAD VISUALS

S1-S20

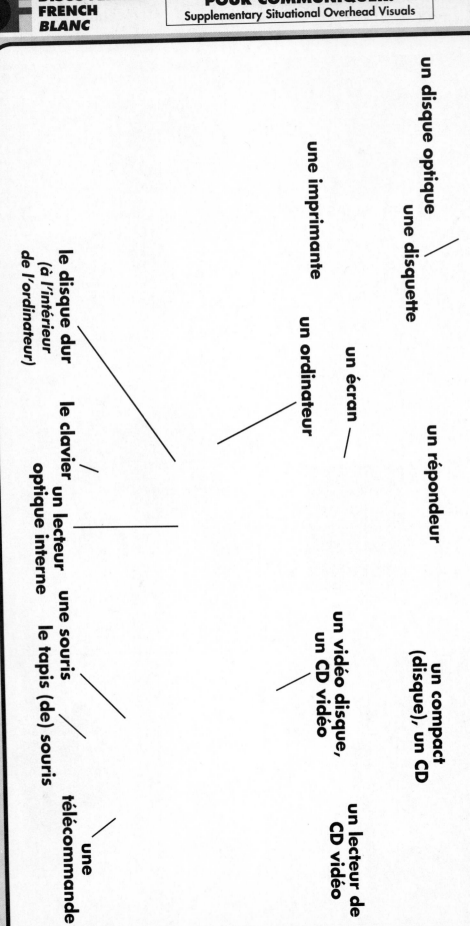

un lecteur optique externe

un disque optique

une disquette

une imprimante

un ordinateur

un écran

un répondeur

le disque dur
(à l'intérieur de l'ordinateur)

le clavier

un lecteur optique interne

une souris

le tapis (de) souris

un vidéo disque, un CD vidéo

un compact (disque), un CD

un lecteur de CD vidéo

un casque

une télécommande

DISCOVERING
FRENCH
BLANC

POUR COMMUNIQUER:
Supplementary Situational Overhead Visuals

Une classe des internautes

S2

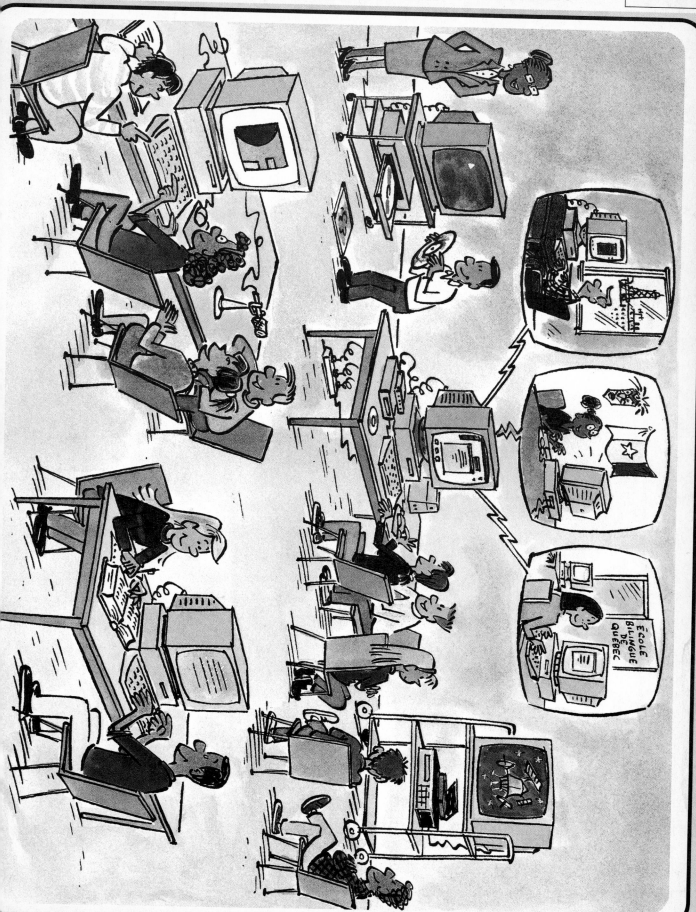

un vidéo disque,
un CD vidéo

un lecteur de
CD vidéo

l'écran
un lecteur
optique
externe

Il enregistre sa voix.

un disque
optique

une station de
travail informatique

Ils correspondent par
courrier électronique.

un magnétoscope

Elle regard un clip vidéo.

Elle recherche l'information.

Il tape un devoir
sur traitement
de texte.

Isabelle

Jean-Claude

Roger

Patrick

Jean-Pierre

Stéphanie

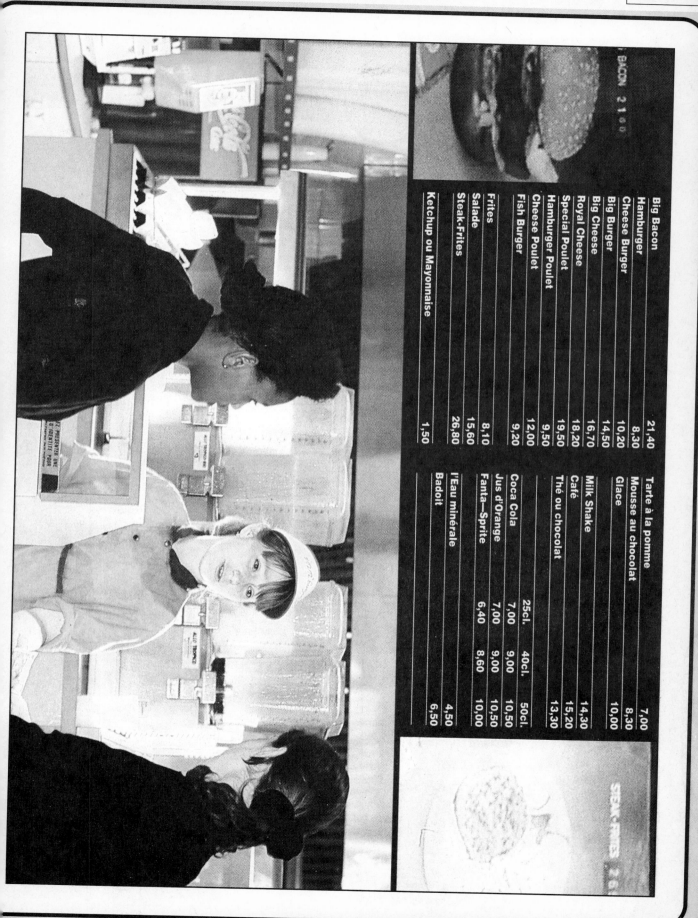

	25cl.	40cl.	50cl.
Big Bacon			21,40
Hamburger			8,30
Cheese Burger			10,20
Big Burger			14,50
Big Cheese			16,70
Royal Cheese			18,20
Special Poulet			19,50
Hamburger Poulet			9,50
Cheese Poulet			12,00
Fish Burger			9,20
Frites			8,10
Salade			15,60
Steak-Frites			26,80
Ketchup ou Mayonnaise			1,50

Tarte à la pomme		7,00
Mousse au chocolat		8,30
Glace		10,00

	25cl.	40cl.	50cl.
Milk Shake			14,30
Café			15,20
Thé ou chocolat			13,30
Coca Cola	7,00	9,00	10,50
Jus d'Orange	7,00	9,00	10,50
Fanta–Sprite	6,40	8,60	10,00
l'Eau minérale			4,50
Badoit			6,50

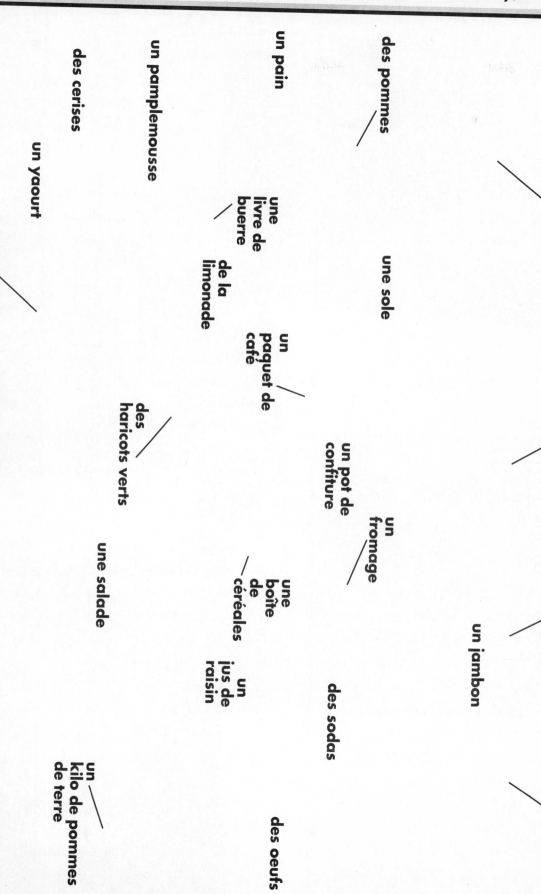

des pommes

un pain

un pamplemousse

des cerises

un yaourt

une bouteille
d'eau minérale

un pot
de mayonnaise

une
livre de
buerre

de la
limonade

un
paquet de
café

des
haricots verts

des bananes

un litre
de lait

une bôite de thon

un
kilo de pommes
de terre

une salade

une
boîte
de
céréales

un
jus de
raisin

des oeufs

une sole

un pot de
confiture

un
fromage

des sodas

un sac d'oranges

un poulet

un jambon

des
carottes

du ketchup

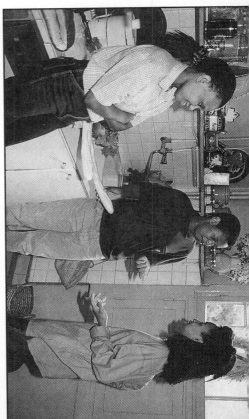

DISCOVERING
FRENCH
BLANC

POUR COMMUNIQUER:
Supplementary Situational Overhead Visuals

Au grand magasin

SAMARITAINE

SAMARITAINE

MONOPRIX
UNIPRIX
On pense à vous tous les

GALERIES Lafayette

Carrefour

Printemps

31, rue Joubert - 75009 Paris

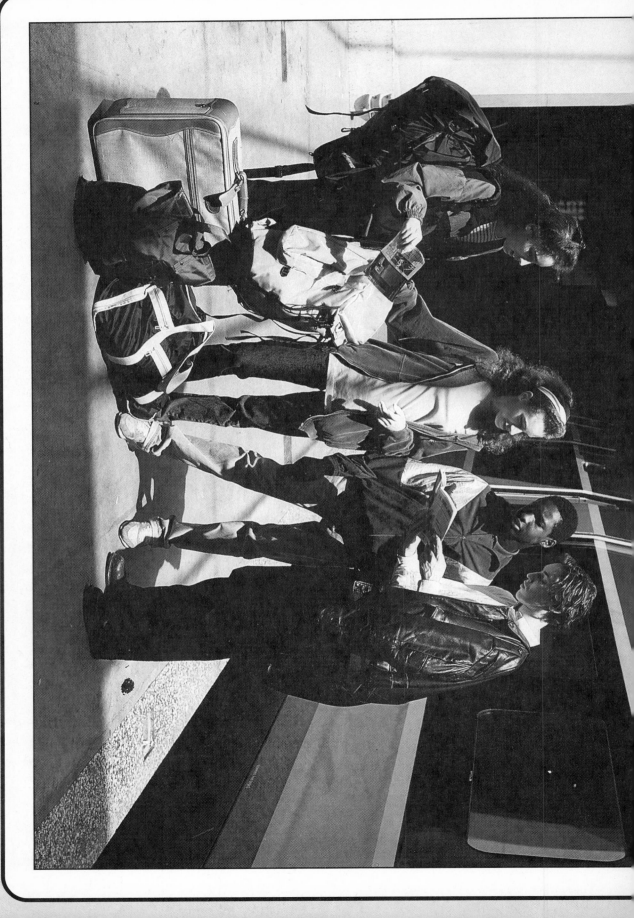

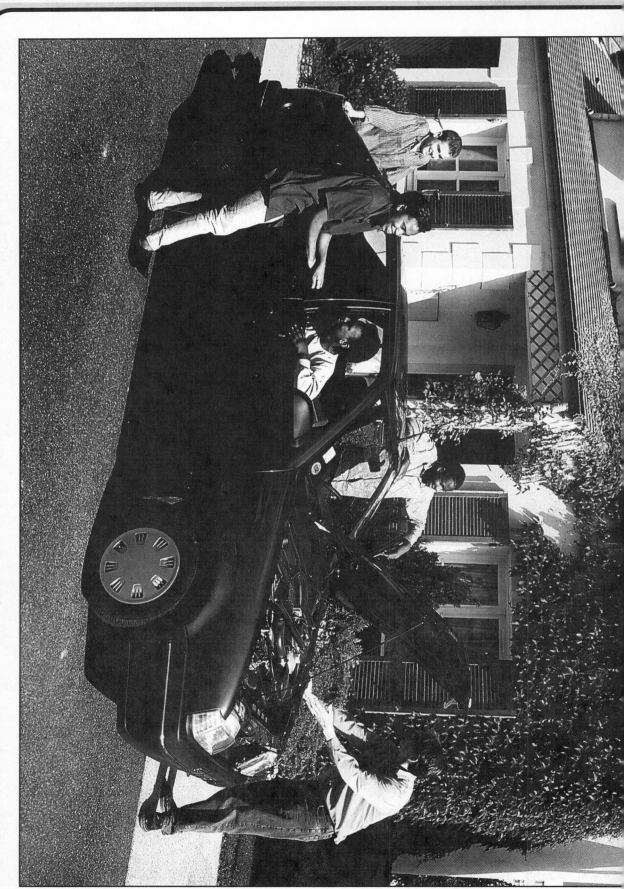

DISCOVERING FRENCH
BLANC

OVERHEAD VISUALS

1-68
Appendix: R

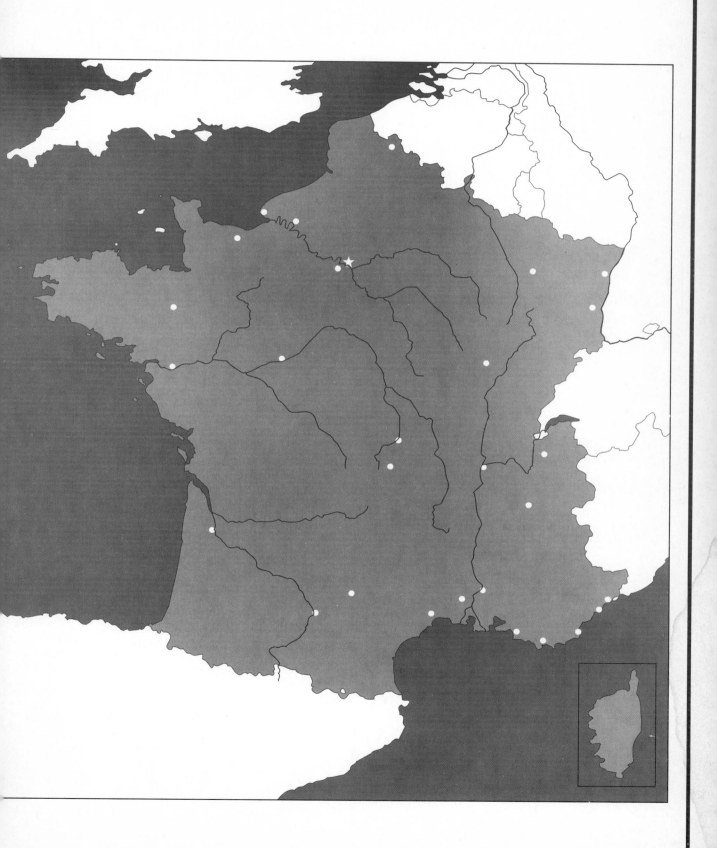

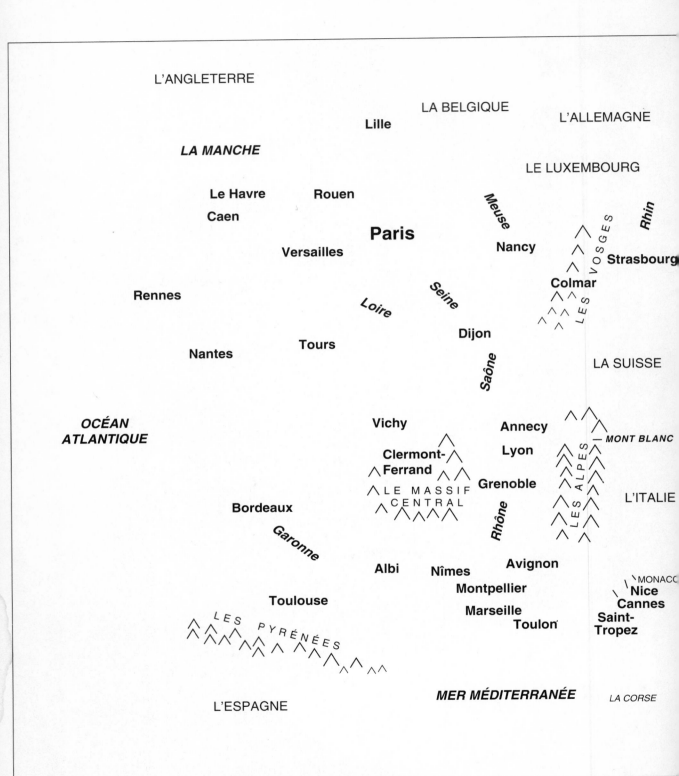

L'ANGLETERRE

LA BELGIQUE

L'ALLEMAGNE

Lille

LE LUXEMBOURG

LA MANCHE

Le Havre

Rouen

Meuse

Rhin

Caen

Paris

Nancy

VOSGES

Strasbourg

Versailles

Colmar

LES

Rennes

Seine

Loire

Dijon

LA SUISSE

Nantes

Tours

Saône

OCÉAN ATLANTIQUE

Vichy

Annecy

— MONT BLANC

Clermont-Ferrand

Lyon

LES ALPES

LE MASSIF CENTRAL

Grenoble

L'ITALIE

Bordeaux

Rhône

Garonne

Albi

Nîmes

Avignon

MONACO

Montpellier

Nice

Toulouse

Marseille

Cannes

Toulon

Saint-Tropez

LES PYRÉNÉES

L'ESPAGNE

MER MÉDITERRANÉE

LA CORSE

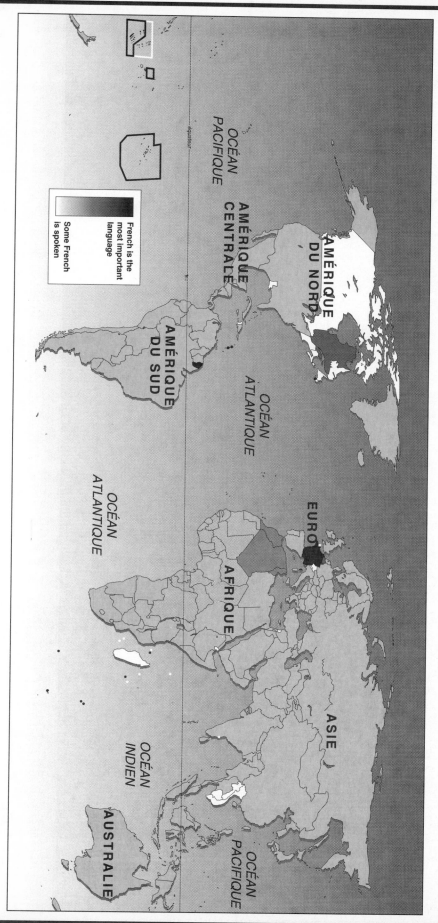

OCÉAN PACIFIQUE

AMÉRIQUE CENTRALE

AMÉRIQUE DU NORD

AMÉRIQUE DU SUD

équateur

OCÉAN ATLANTIQUE

OCÉAN ATLANTIQUE

EUROPE

AFRIQUE

ASIE

OCÉAN INDIEN

OCÉAN PACIFIQUE

AUSTRALIE

French is the most important language

Some French is spoken

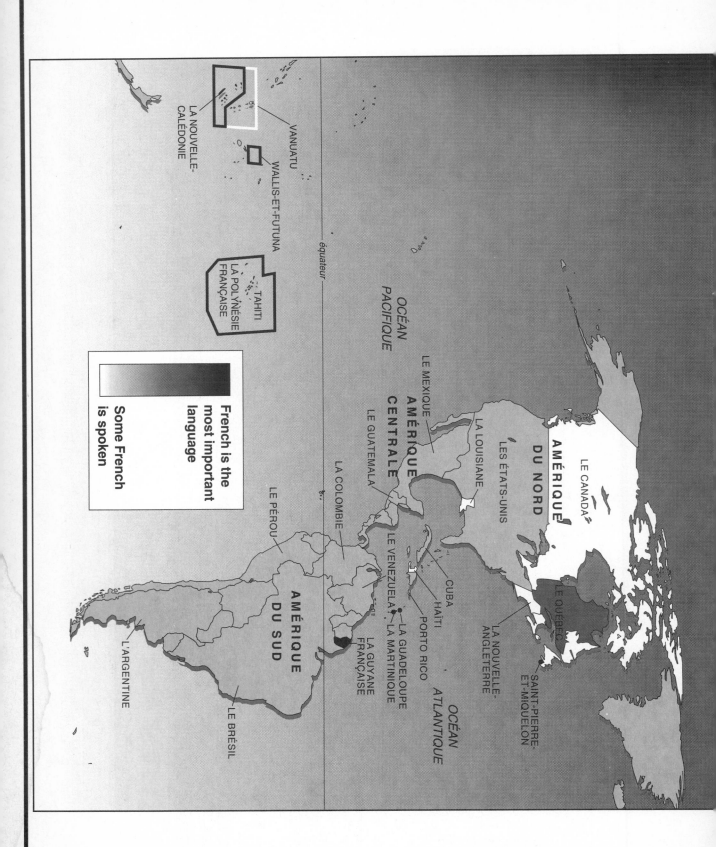

LA NOUVELLE-
CALÉDONIE

VANUATU

WALLIS-ET-FUTUNA

LA POLYNÉSIE
FRANÇAISE

TAHITI

équateur

French is the
most important
language

Some French
is spoken

OCÉAN
PACIFIQUE

LE MEXIQUE

AMÉRIQUE
CENTRALE

LE GUATEMALA

LA COLOMBIE

LE PÉROU

AMÉRIQUE
DU SUD

L'ARGENTINE

LE BRÉSIL

LA GUYANE
FRANÇAISE

LA MARTINIQUE

LA GUADELOUPE

LE VENEZUELA

PORTO RICO

HAÏTI

CUBA

OCÉAN
ATLANTIQUE

LA LOUISIANE

LES ÉTATS-UNIS

AMÉRIQUE
DU NORD

LE CANADA

LE QUÉBEC

LA NOUVELLE-
ANGLETERRE

SAINT-PIERRE-
ET-MIQUELON

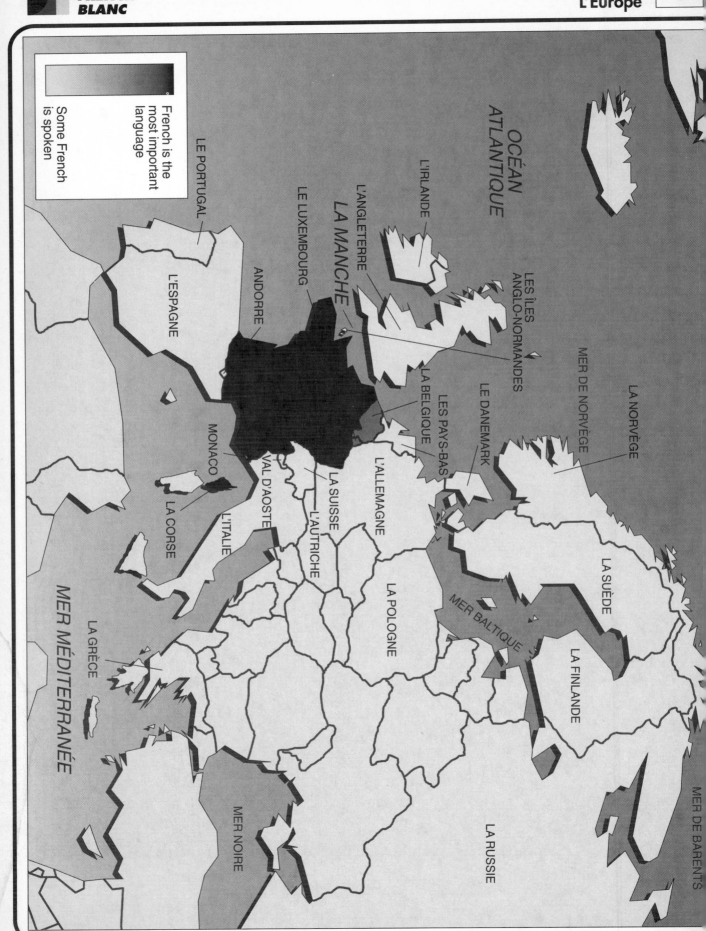

DISCOVERING FRENCH BLANC

Some French is spoken

French is the most important language

OCÉAN ATLANTIQUE

LE PORTUGAL
L'ESPAGNE
ANDORRE
LE LUXEMBOURG
L'ANGLETERRE
LA MANCHE
L'IRLANDE
LES ÎLES ANGLO-NORMANDES
MER DE NORVÈGE
LA NORVÈGE
LA BELGIQUE
LES PAYS-BAS
LE DANEMARK
MONACO
LA CORSE
L'ITALIE
VAL D'AOSTE
L'AUTRICHE
LA SUISSE
L'ALLEMAGNE
LA POLOGNE
LA SUÈDE
MER BALTIQUE
LA FINLANDE
MER MÉDITERRANÉE
LA GRÈCE
MER NOIRE
LA RUSSIE
MER DE BARENTS

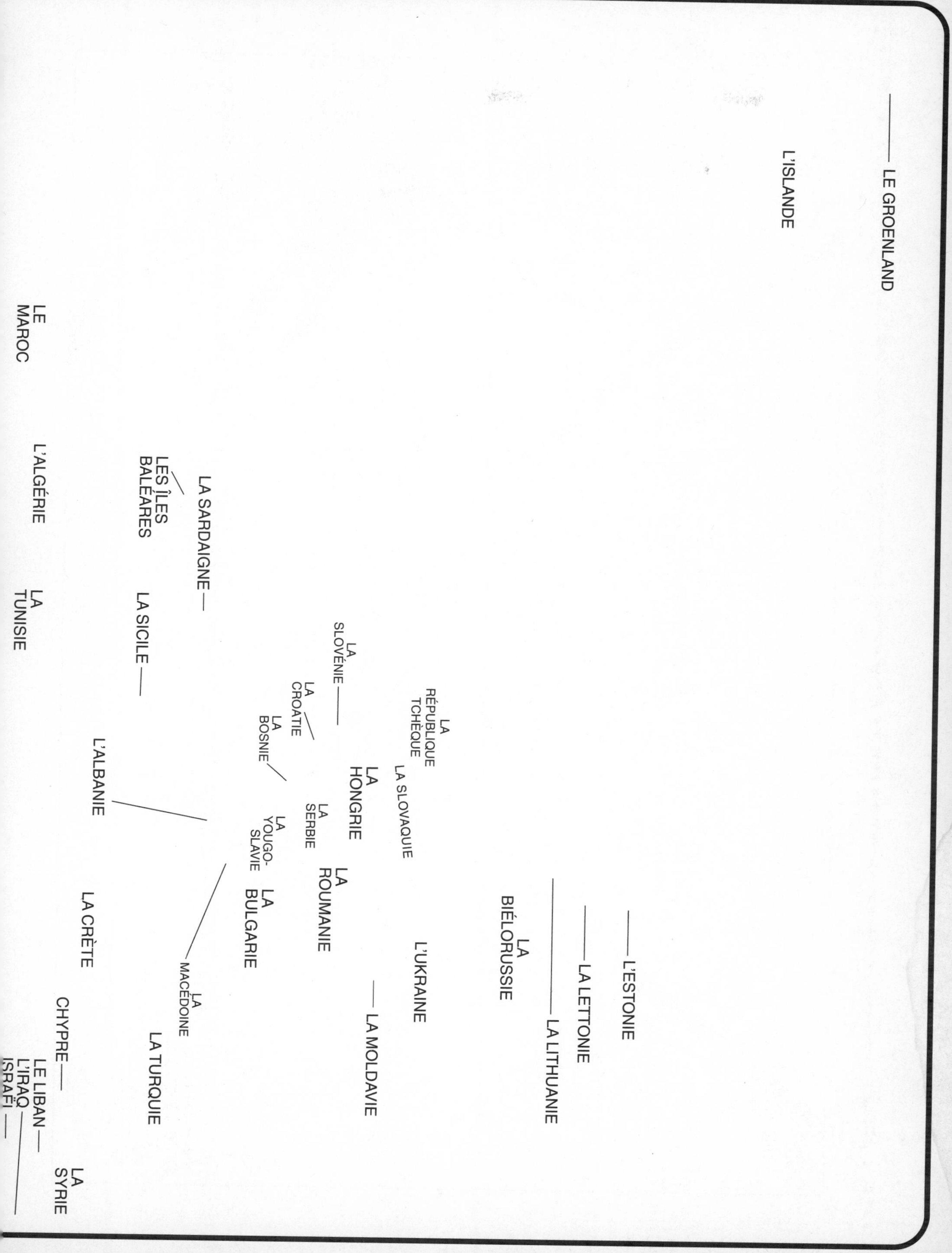

LE GROENLAND

L'ISLANDE

LE MAROC

L'ALGÉRIE

LES ÎLES BALÉARES

LA SARDAIGNE —

LA TUNISIE

LA SICILE —

LA SLOVÉNIE —

LA CROATIE

LA BOSNIE

LA RÉPUBLIQUE TCHÈQUE

LA SLOVAQUIE

LA HONGRIE

L'ALBANIE

LA SERBIE

LA YOUGO-SLAVIE

LA ROUMANIE

LA BULGARIE

LA BIÉLORUSSIE

LA LETTONIE

L'ESTONIE

LA CRÈTE

LA MACÉDOINE

L'UKRAINE

LA MOLDAVIE

LA LITHUANIE

CHYPRE —

LA TURQUIE

LE LIBAN —
L'IRAQ
ISRAËl —

LA SYRIE

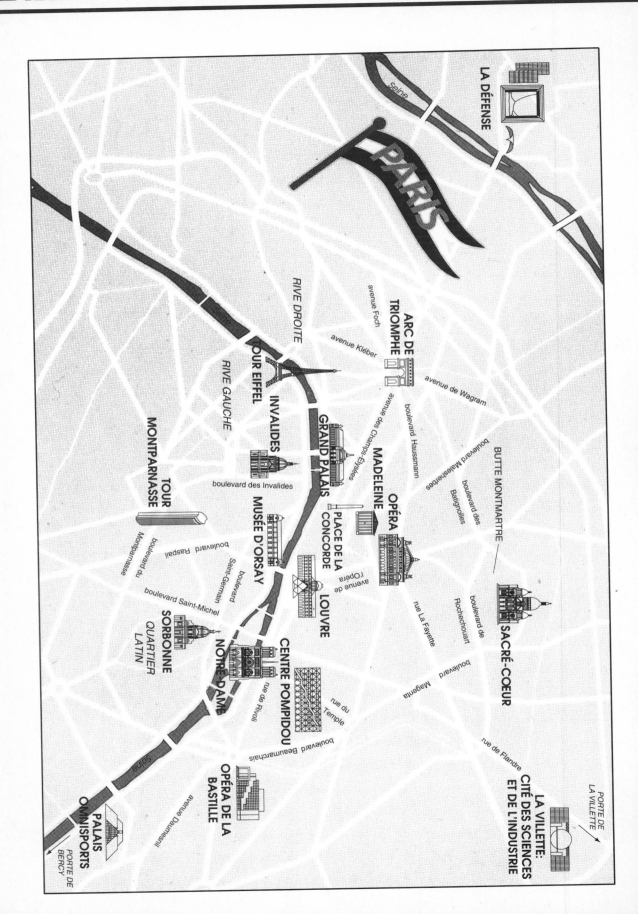

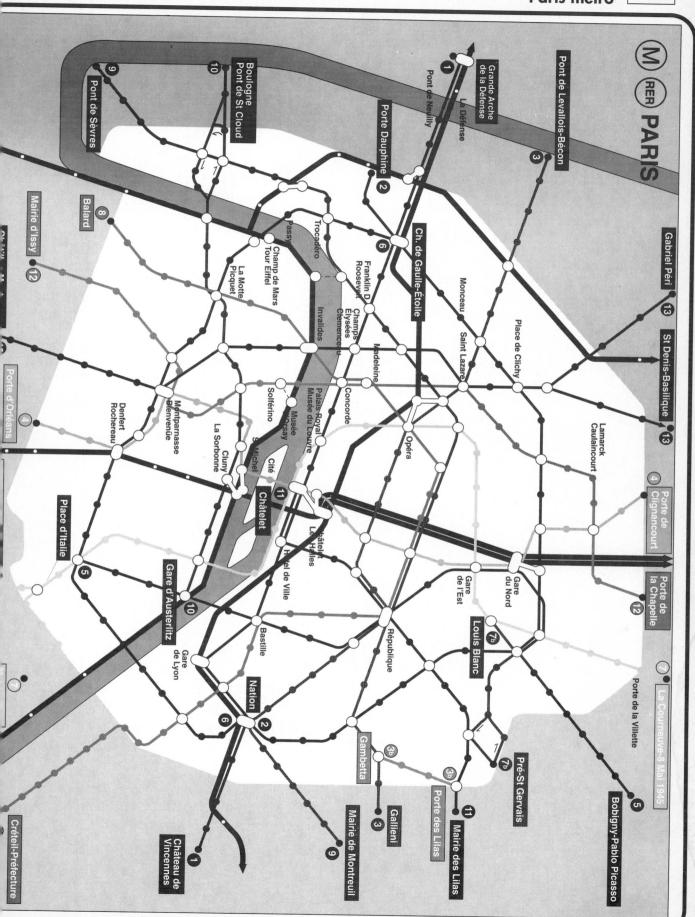

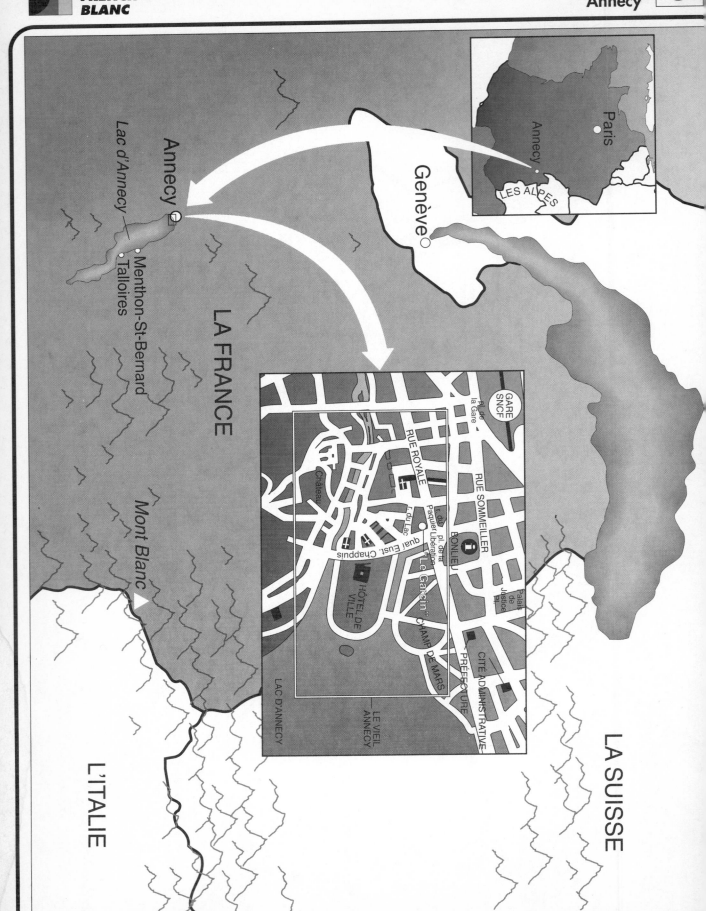

la valise de Marc

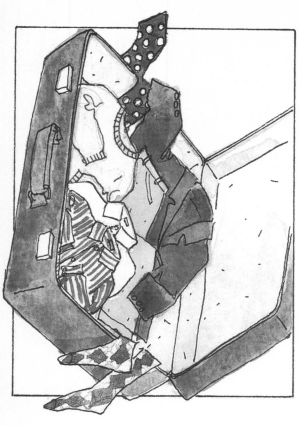

le bureau de Michèle

la valise de Caroline

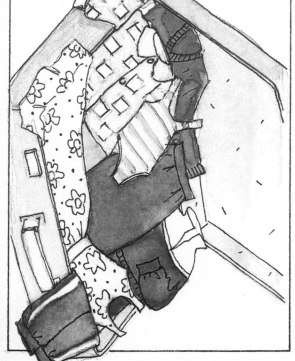

la chambre de Philippe

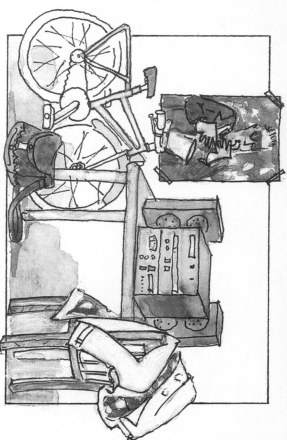

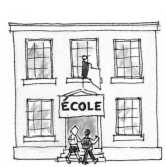

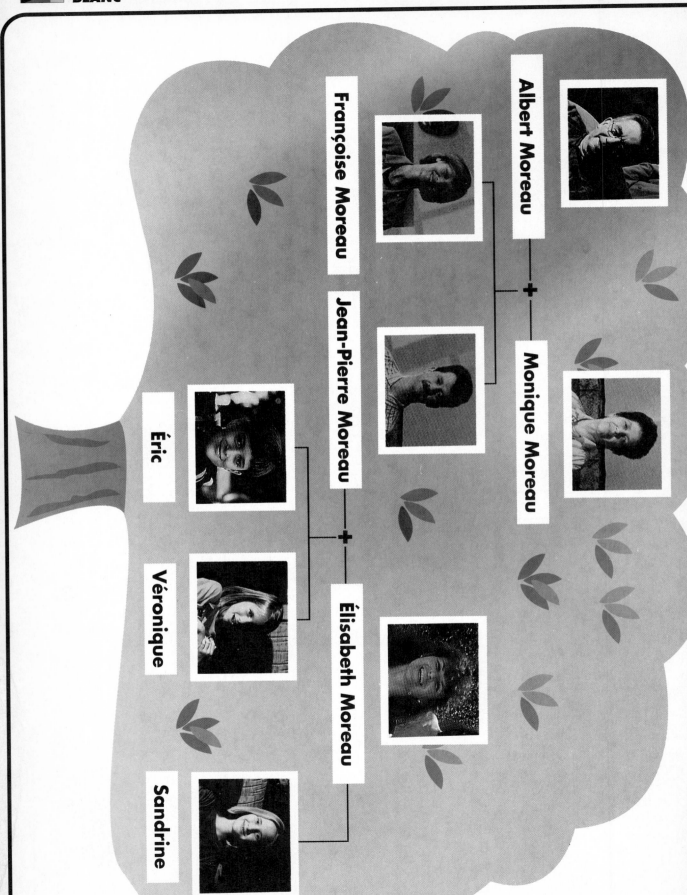

Albert Moreau

Françoise Moreau

Monique Moreau

Jean-Pierre Moreau

Éric

Véronique

Élisabeth Moreau

Sandrine

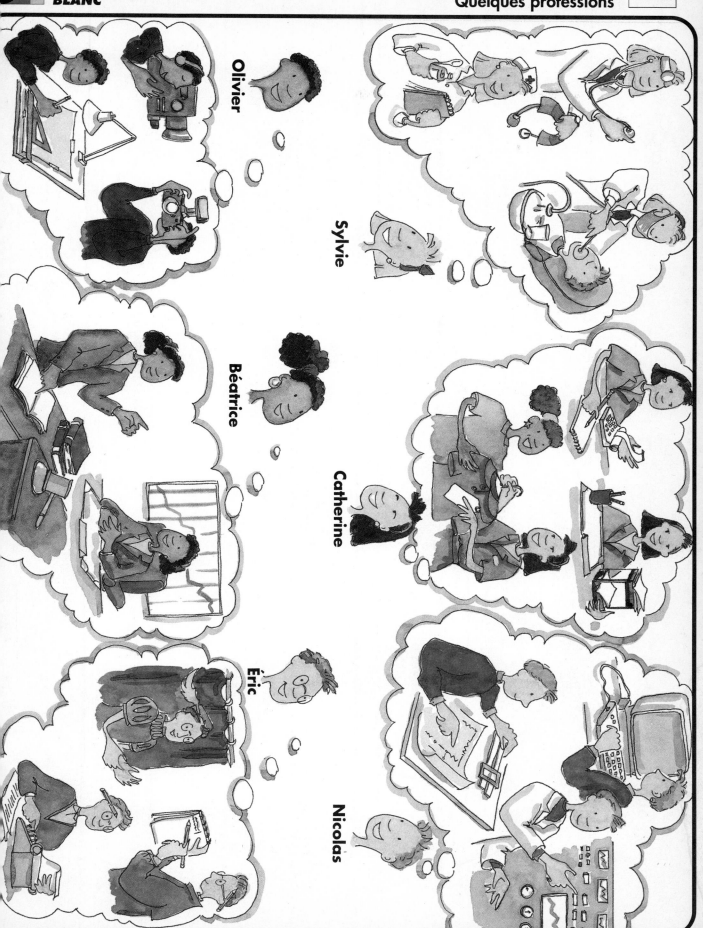

Olivier

Sylvie

Béatrice

Catherine

Éric

Nicolas

Philippe

Isabelle

Malice

Henri

Mme Camus

Mlle Martin

M. Duval

Éric

Simon

Philippe

Alice

Henri

Jacques

Mlle Dumas

M. Mercier

Louise

Pierre

Lucie et Georges

Paul

Florence et Denise

Christine

Mme Jabot

Pierre

Alain

Lucie

David

Sophie

Robert

Hélène

Paul

Éric

Sylvie

Nathalie

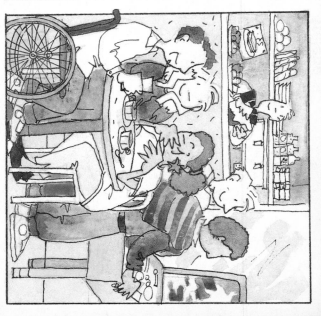

On reste à la maison . . .

Où allez-vous passer le weekend?

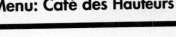

$\frac{M}{^\circ O}$ Café des Hauteurs

Les consommations

Vittel (25 cl)	11,00
Perrier (20 cl)	12,00
Sodas et Tonics (20 cl)	13,00
Supplément Sirop	3,00

Les jus de fruits et nectars (bouteille 20 cl)

Orange, pamplemousse, abricot, poire, tomate, ananas	15,00

Les jus de fruits pressés

Orange, pamplemousse, citron	16,50

Les cafés

Café pur arabica	6,30
Café décaféiné	6,70
Café crème	10,00

Les chocolats chauds

Chocolat	12,00
Chocolat à la canelle	13,00

Les thés

Earl Grey	13,50
Chine	13,50

Les salades composées

SALADE ANTIBOISE	24,00
Thon, tomates, oeuf dur, anchois, salade, riz.	
SALADE FLASH	20,50
Salade, jambon blanc, blanc de poulet, fromage.	
SALADE VEGETARIENNE	24,00
SALADE VERTE	15,00

Les sandwichs

Baguette jambon blanc	15,50
Pain niçois	26,00
Thon, tomates, salade, oeuf dur, mayonnaise.	
Baguette fromage	18,50
Baguette jambon blanc, fromage	21,00

Les pâtisseries

Croissant au beurre	6,70
Pain au chocolat	8,80
Tarte aux pommes	21,50
Tarte Citron	27,00
Brownies au chocolat et noix de pécan	26,00

Glace

3 boules au choix: vanille, chocolat, citron vert	19,50

Service 15% compris

Pour le petit déjeuner

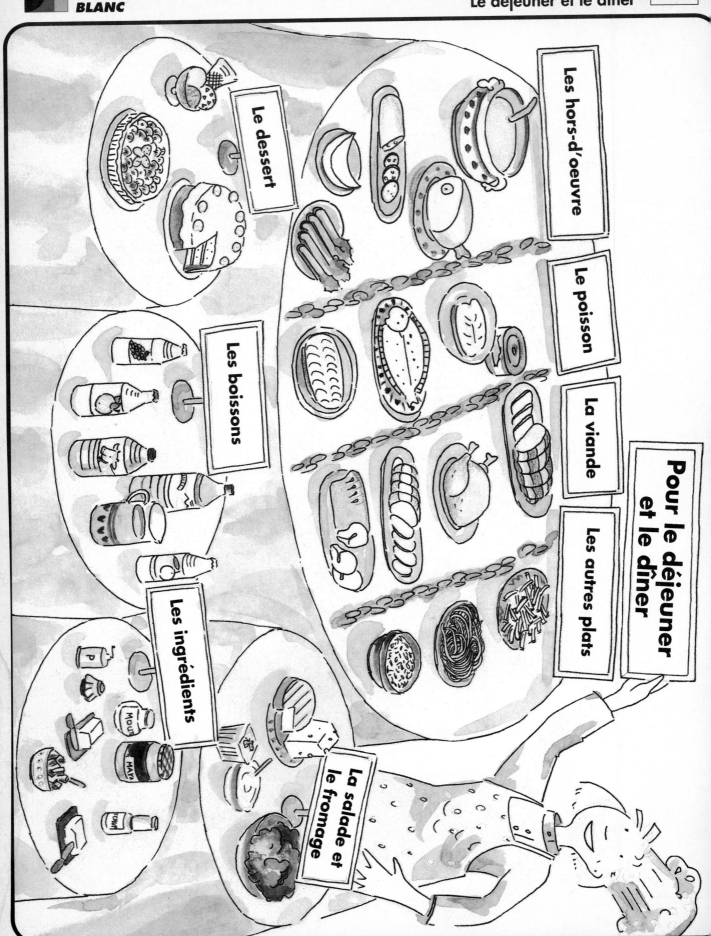

Voici...

un poulet

un melon

une salade

une tarte

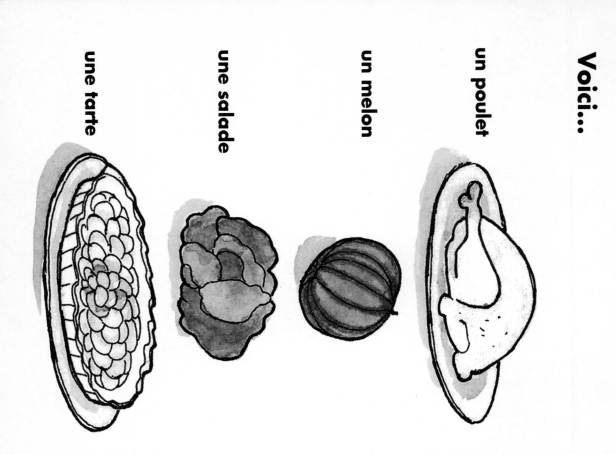

Voilà...

du poulet

du melon

de la salade

de la tarte

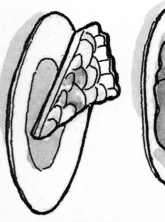
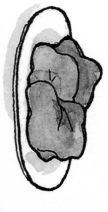
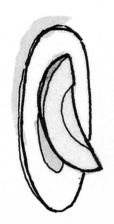

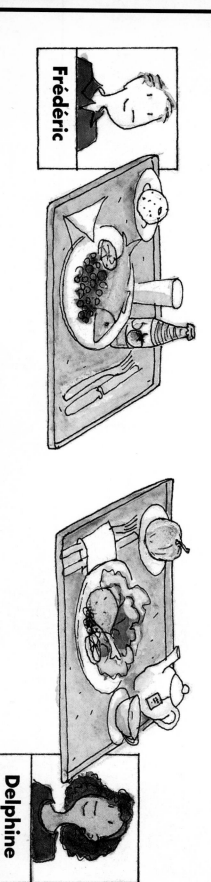

Frédéric

Christine

Guillaume

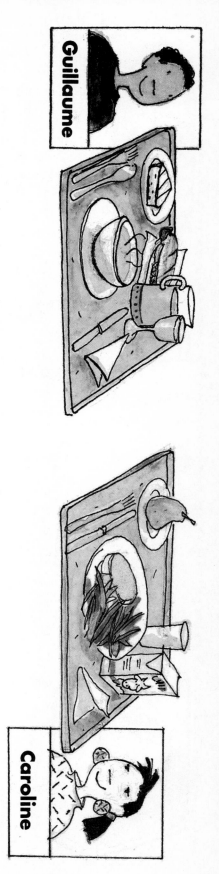

Delphine

Caroline

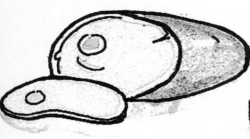

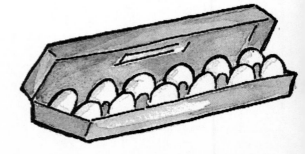

Jean-Pierre

Guy

Claire

DISCOVERING FRENCH BLANC

Paul et François

des jeunes

André et Claire

Sylvie et Marc

Monique et Georges

ON LIT...

ON ÉCRIT...

ON DIT...

Michèle

Pierre

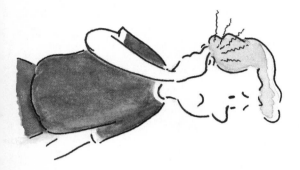

M. Dupont

Hélène

Alain

Sylvie

Paul

Marie

François

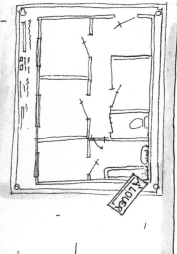

AGENCE IMMOBILIÈRE
La Résidence

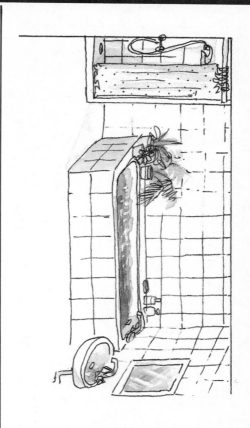

Alain   Lucie

Maintenant . . .

Avant . . .

DISCOVERING FRENCH BLANC

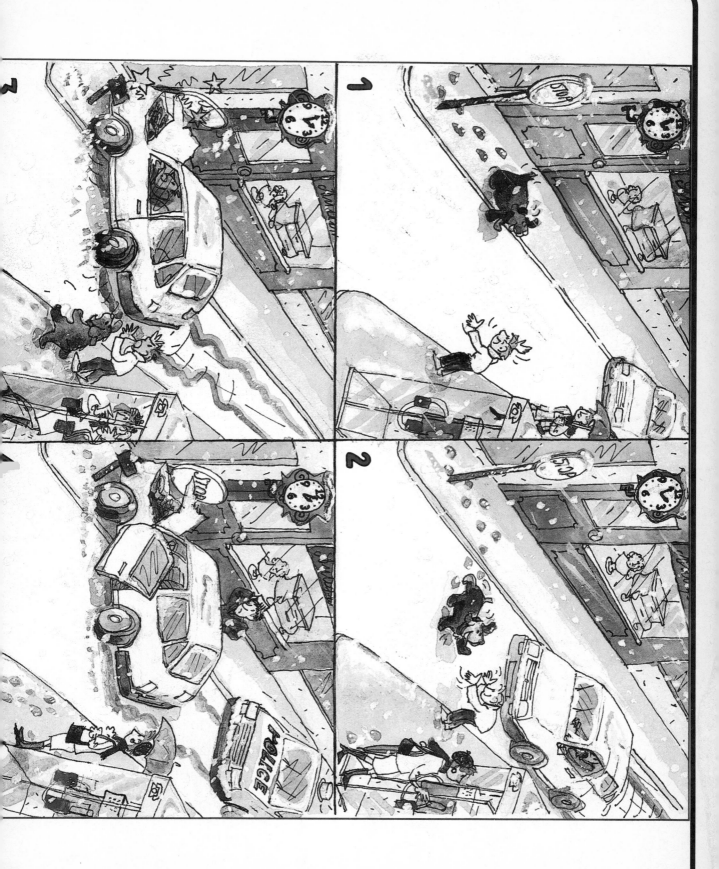

Pour hommes et femmes

Pour femmes

Pour hommes

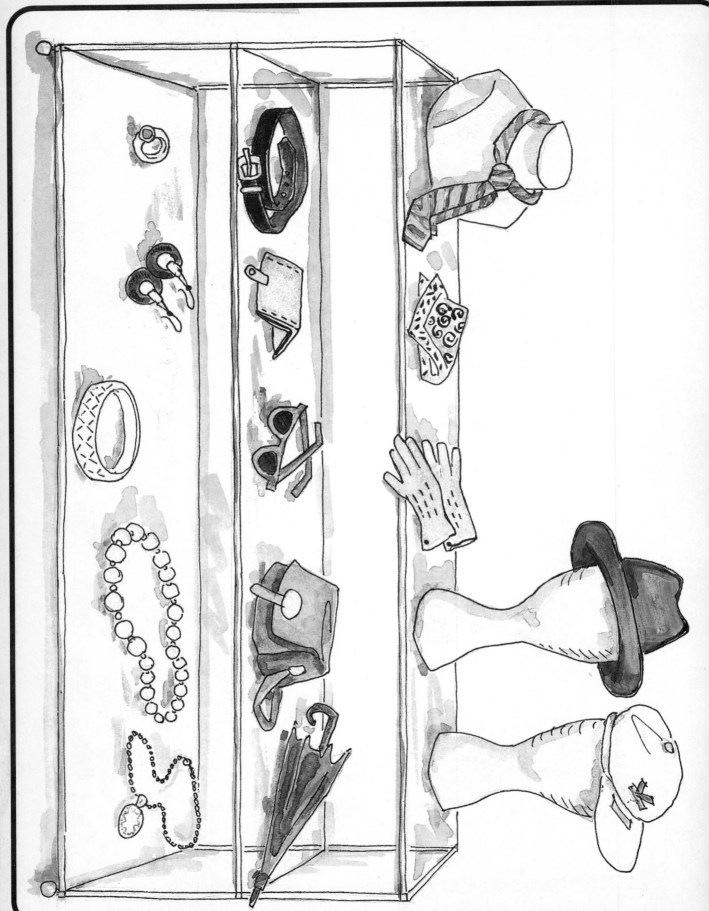

**DISCOVERING
FRENCH
BLANC**

Les accessoires et
les articles personnels *(overlay)*

55(o)

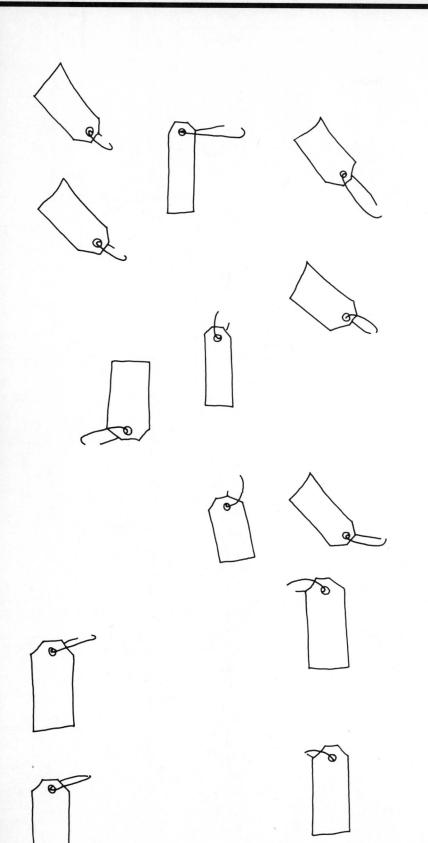
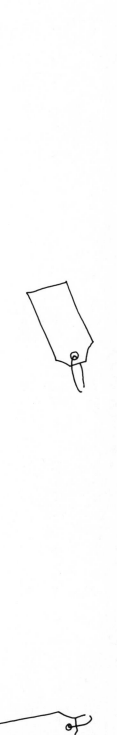

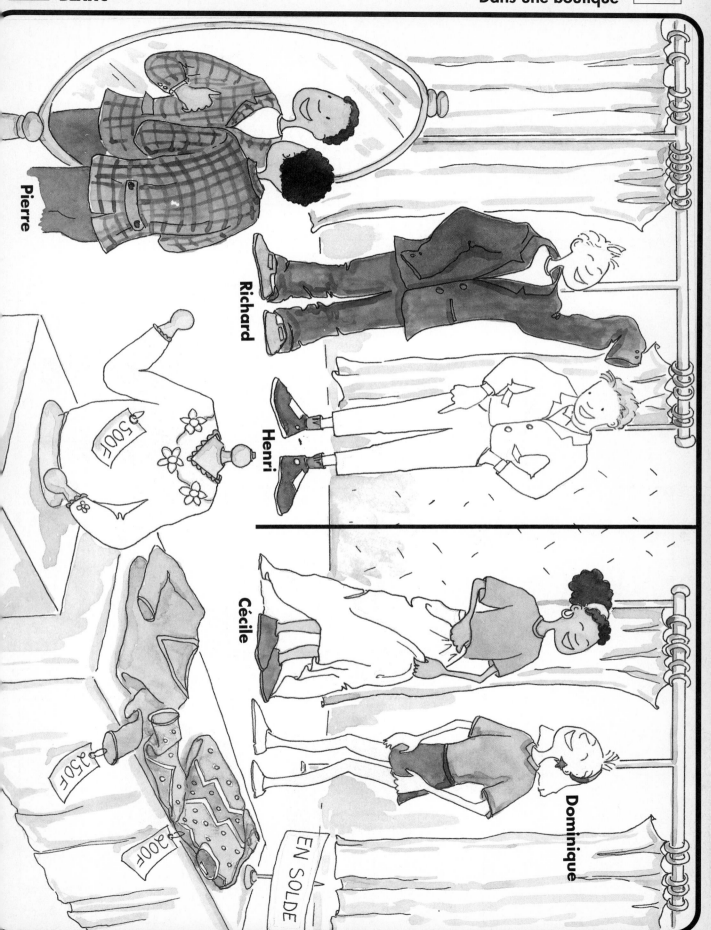

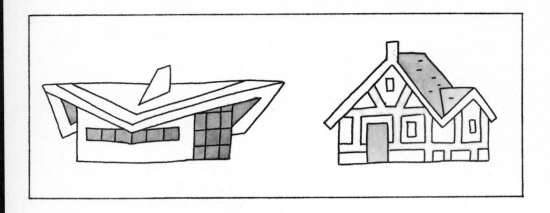

Paul

Marie

Alice

M. Masson

André

Monique

Claire

Roger

Juliette

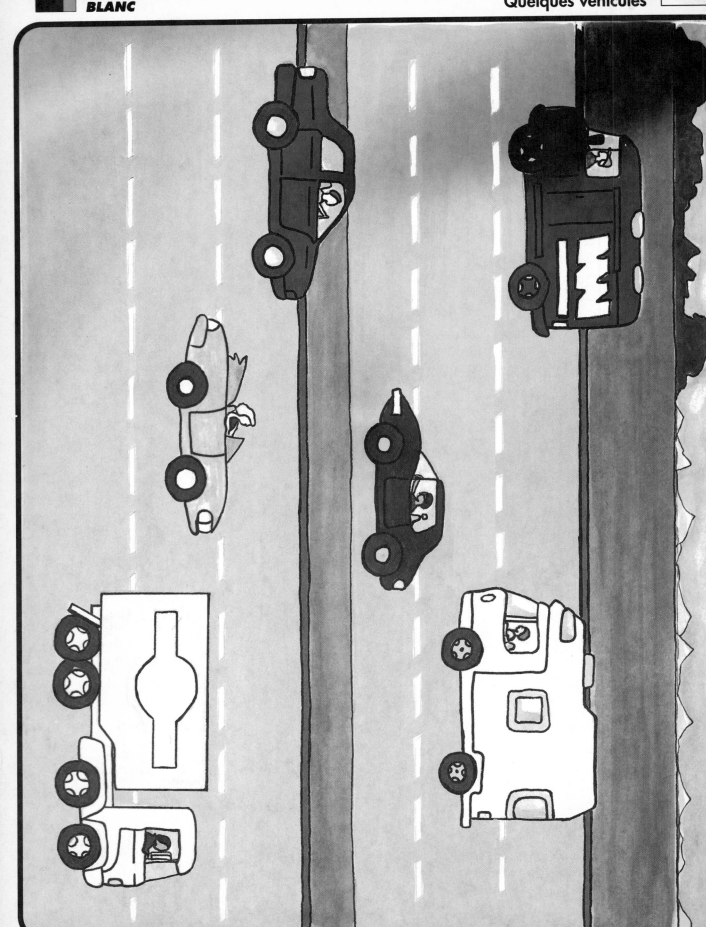

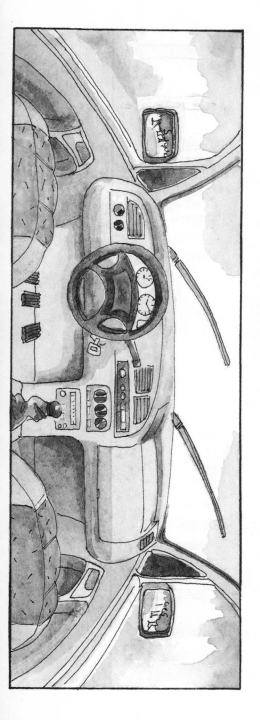

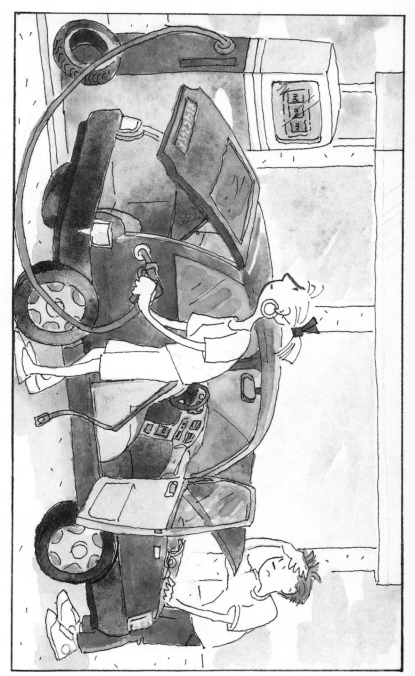

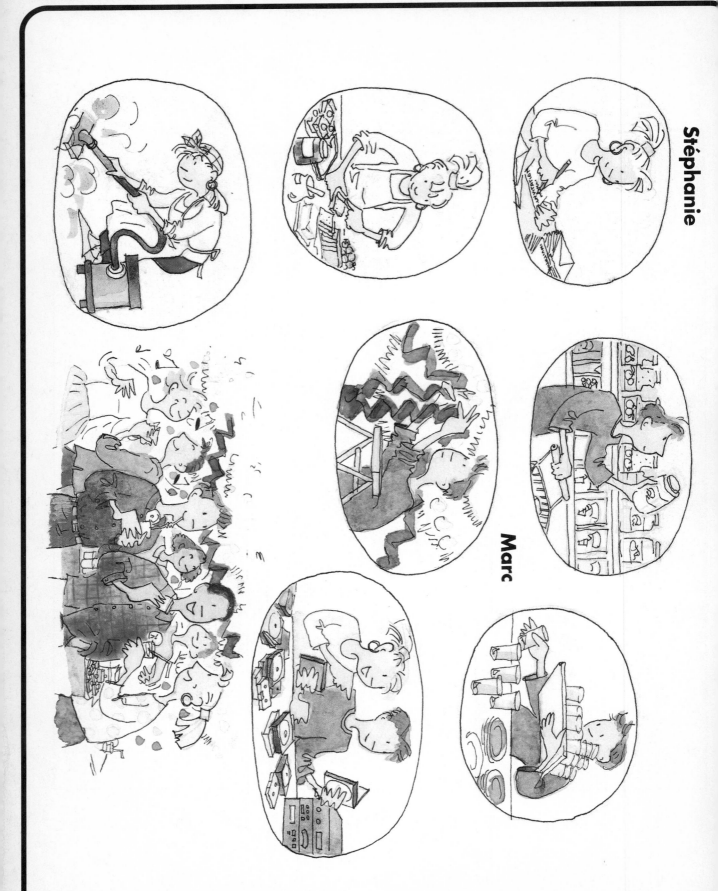

Stéphanie

Marc

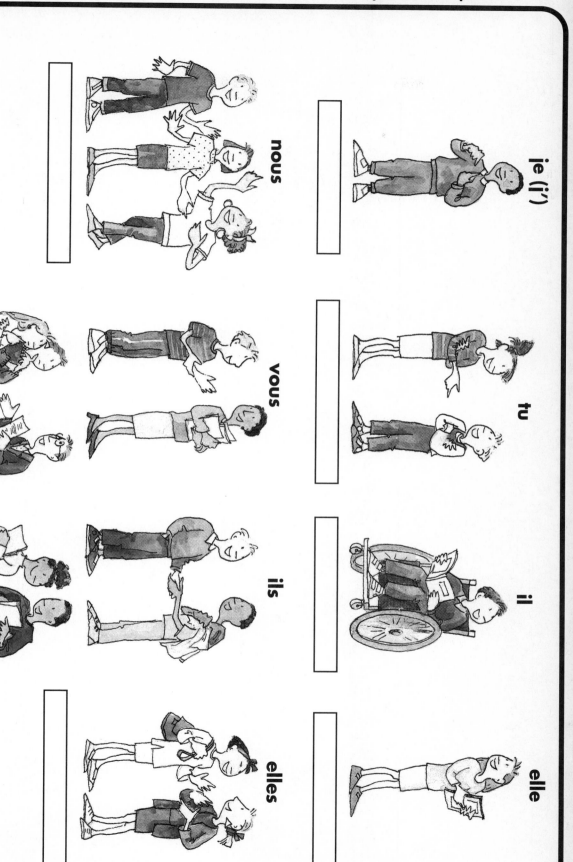

nous

je (j')

vous

tu

ils

il

elles

elle

DISCOVERING FRENCH

BLANC

SUGGESTED EXPANSION ACTIVITIES

Contents

**Blanc
Overhead
Visuals**

Contents—Suggested Expansion Activities (continued)

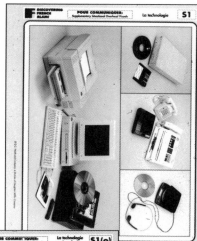

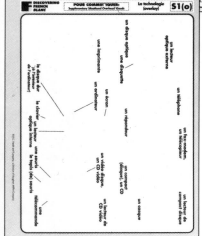

DESCRIPTION

Labelled photographs of communication technology:

un lecteur optique externe	**une imprimante**
un disque optique	**un ordinateur**
une disquette	**un écran**
	un lecteur optique interne
un téléphone	**le disque dur**
un répondeur	**le clavier**
un fax-modem/ un télécopieur	
	un vidéo disque/ un CD vidéo
un lecteur de compact disque	**un lecteur de CD vidéo**
un casque	**une télécommande**
un compact (disque)/ un CD	**une souris**
	le tapis (de) souris

MEETING NATIONAL STANDARDS

GOAL 3:
CONNECTIONS

STANDARD 3.1
Using French to further one's knowledge: computer technology

After practicing the new vocabulary with the transparency, have students identify computer compents in French:

- [RECOGNITION] *(pointing to the monitor)*
  - **Est-ce que c'est le clavier? Non.]**
  - **Est-ce que c'est l'écran? [Oui.]**
- [PRODUCTION] *(pointing to the mouse)*
  - **Qu'est-ce que c'est?**
    [C'est la souris.]

Nommez les différents éléments d'un ordinateur.

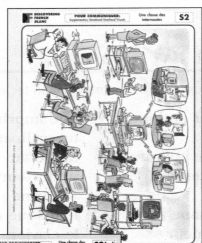

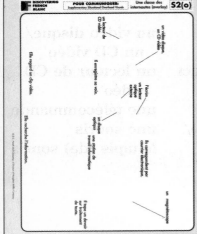

DESCRIPTION

Labelled illustration of a high-tech classroom.

un vidéo disque, un CD vidéo *video disc*

un lecteur de CD vidéo *video disc player*

un lecteur optique externe *external CD-ROM drive*

un disque optique *CD-ROM*

un station de travail informatique *computer works...*

un magnétoscope *VCR, video cassette recorder*

enregistrer sa voix *to record one's voice*
il enregistre sa voix.

regarder un clip vidéo *to watch a video clip*
Elle regard un clip vidéo.

rechercher l'information *to do research, look for in...*
Elle recherche l'information.

correspondre par courrier électronique *to corres...*
by e-mail
Ils correspondent par courrier électronique

taper un devoir [sur traitement de texte] *to do*
wordprocessing [homework]
Il tape un devoir sur traitement de texte.

ADDITIONAL TERMS

le curseur *the cursor*

un microphone *microphone*

les articles *on-screen menu items*

taper *to type*

cliquer *to click (with the mouse)*

accéder à des fichiers *to access files*

écouter un morceau de musique [morceau son...
to hear a music clip [audio clip]

GOAL 3:
CONNECTIONS

STANDARD 3.1
Using French to further one's knowledge:
computer technology

After practicing the new vocabulary with
the transparency, have students identify
computer compents in French:

- [RECOGNITION] *(pointing to the work station)*
  - **Est-ce que c'est un vidéo
    disque? [Non.]**
  - **Est-ce que c'est un station de
    travail informatique? [Oui.]**
- [PRODUCTION] *(pointing to the work station)*
  - **Qu'est-ce que c'est? [C'est un
    station de travail informatique.]**

*Nommez les différents éléments
d'un ordinateur.*

S3   En famille

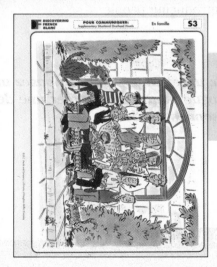

DESCRIPTION

Drawing of a large family gathering with grandparents,
parents, children and pets.

REVIEW AND PRACTICE

CORRELATION: UNIT 1
(theme: introducing people)

Leçon 1 p. T32; pp. T34-T35
Leçon 2 pp. T47-T48
Leçon 3 p. T56
see also: **Visuals 13,15**

Have the class give names to all the family members. Write this on the Visual with a washable marker.

- Review words referring to family members: e.g., **le grand-père, le fils,** etc.
- Review the way the French introduce people, p. 38.

Donnez un nom à chaque membre de la famille.

MEETING NATIONAL STANDARDS

GOAL 1:
COMMUNICATION

STANDARD 1.1
Interpersonal Communication: Introducing people

Have pairs of students invent conversations in which one introduces to the other someone depicted on the Visual.

Avec un(e) camarade, composez un dialogue pour lui présenter une des personnes du dessin.

MEETING NATIONAL STANDARDS

GOAL 1:
COMMUNICATION

STANDARD 1.1
Interpersonal Communication: Engaging in conversation

Have pairs of students imagine conversations between two people in the visual.

Avec un(e) camarade, imaginez un dialogue entre deux personnes du dessin.

GOAL 1:	STANDARD 1.3
COMMUNICATION	Presentational Communication: Oral descriptions

Have students pick one of the people in the visual, and describe his/her name, age, relationship to others in the picture, etc.

Choisissez une des personnes du dessin, et décrivez cette personne (nom, âge, et la relation familiale).

S4 Au téléphone

DESCRIPTION

A photo-montage of 6 people phoning.

Jean-Claude
Patrick
Stéphanie
Isabelle
Roger
Jean-Pierre

REVIEW AND PRACTICE

CORRELATION: UNIT 1 *(theme: making phone calls)*	Leçon 1 pp. T38-T39 Leçon 23 p. T322 *see also:* Visuals 19-21, 35, 36, 51

Review French expressions used in making phone calls, p. 38.

Révisez les expressions utilisées au téléphone.

CORRELATION: UNIT 4 *(theme: extending invitations)*	Leçon 13 pp. T194-T199

Review French expressions used in making invitations, pp. 198-199.

Révisez les expressions utilisées pour inviter quelqu'un.

MEETING NATIONAL STANDARDS

GOAL 1:
COMMUNICATION

STANDARD 1.1
Interpersonal Communication:
Engaging in phone conversations

Have pairs of students imagine
conversations between two people in
the visual, or between one of the people
in the visual and someone else.

*Avec un(e) camarade, imaginez un dialogue
entre deux personnes de la photo, ou entre
une personne de la photo et une autre
personne.*

MEETING NATIONAL STANDARDS

GOAL 1:
COMMUNICATION

STANDARD 1.1
Interpersonal Communication:
Extending invitations

Have pairs of students imagine
conversations in which one of the
people in the visual is phoning a friend to
make plans to go out together. The first
suggestion does not work out, and the
friend refuses politely. A second suggestion
leads to a date.

*Une personne de la photo téléphone à
un(e) ami(e) pour faire des projets pour
sortir ensemble. L'ami(e) refuse poliment la
première suggestion. Une deuxième
suggestion a pour résultat un rendez-vous.
Jouez ce dialogue avec un(e) camarade.*

DESCRIPTION

Photo of two girls looking at a Paris metro map.

Note: If you wish, have students assign French names to the young people in this transparency.

REVIEW AND PRACTICE

CORRELATION: UNIT 2
(theme: weekend in Paris)

Leçon 5	pp. T96-T99	Leçon 7	p. T119
Leçon 13	p. T194	Leçon 18	p. T264
Leçon 21	p. T305	Leçon 22	p. T309

see also: **Visuals 4a, 4b, 9, 18,**

MEETING NATIONAL STANDARDS

GOAL 1:
COMMUNICATION

STANDARD 1.1
Interpersonal Communication:
Engaging in conversation

Students invent a conversation between the two girls in the visual who are planning to visit Paris. Where will they go? What monuments do they want to photograph? Etc.

Inventez un dialogue entre les deux filles qui veulent visiter Paris: Où vont-elles aller? Quels monuments veulent-elles photographier?

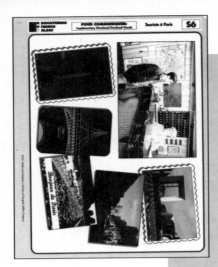

DESCRIPTION

Main photo shows a boy at a hotel reception desk. Five postcards suggest places he might want to visit:

- **L'Arche de la Défense**
- **L'Arc de Triomphe et les Champs-Élysées**
- **La place de la Bastille**
- **La tour Eiffel**
- **Le Jardin des Tuileries**

Note: If you wish, have students assign French names to the people in this transparency.

REVIEW AND PRACTICE

CORRELATION: UNIT 2
   (theme: weekend in Paris)

Leçon 6	pp. T104-T110
Leçon 7	pp. T116-T121
Leçon 8	pp. T126-T131
Leçon 13	pp. T192-T195
Leçon 16	p. T225
Interlude 4	pp. T234-T239
Leçon 31	pp. T420-T421; p. T423; pp. T428-T429

see also: **Visuals 4a, 4b, 18, 19, 21, 25, 35, 39**

MEETING NATIONAL STANDARDS

GOAL 1:
   CCOMMUNICATION

STANDARD 1.3
   Presentational Communication: Writing postcards

Students pick one of the postcards and write a short message to a friend. For example, they might mention when they arrived in Paris, what they have been doing, etc.

Choisissez une des cartes postales et écrivez un petit message à un(e) ami(e). Par exemple, dites quand vous êtes arrivé(e) à Paris, ce que vous avez fait, etc.

GOAL 1:
COMMUNICATION

STANDARD 1.3
Presentational Communication:
Narrating in the past

Students will describe an imaginary visit to Paris using the passé composé, both **être** and **avoir** verbs. They can indicate whether or not they visited the places illustrated in the visual.

Imaginez que vous avez visité Paris! Décrivez cette visite en utilisant le passé composé (utilisez des verbes avec avoir et être). Vous pouvez dire, par exemple, si oui ou non vous avez visité les endroits montrés sur la photo.

S7 Au Fast-food

DESCRIPTION

Photo showing two young people ordering at a fast-food restaurant.

Note: If you wish, have students assign French names to the young people in this transparency.

Source: Photo similar to that in the Student Text, p. 144.

REVIEW AND PRACTICE

CORRELATION: UNIT 3
(theme: ordering food)

Leçon 3
Leçon 9   pp. T144-T146; p.T148
Leçon 10   p.T156
Leçon 11   pp. T166-T169
Leçon 12   pp. T176-T177

MEETING NATIONAL STANDARDS

GOAL 1:
COMMUNICATION

STANDARD 1.1
Interpersonal Communication:
Ordering food

- Students invent conversations in which they order something to eat and drink.
- Students imagine a conversation between the two young people who are trying to decide what to order.

- *Inventez un dialogue où vous commandez à boire et à manger.*
- *Deux jeunes de la photo décident ce qu'ils veulent commander. Jouez ce dialogue.*

MEETING NATIONAL STANDARDS

GOAL 4:
COMPARISONS

STANDARD 4.2
Comparing American and French culture

Which items on the menu would one also find in an American hamburger place?

Which items on the menu would one not find in an America?

Which names of menu items have been borrowed from English?

Quels éléments du menu peut-on trouver aussi aux États-Unis dans les restaurants où on mange des hamburgers?

Quels éléments du menu est-ce qu'on ne trouve pas aux États-Unis?

Quels éléments du menu ont un nom emprunté (borrowed) à l'anglais?

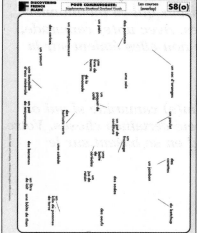

DESCRIPTION

Drawing of a large kitchen table with foods that have just been purchased.

All items are labelled in French on the overlay:

un sac d'oranges	un jus de raisin
un poulet	des oeufs
des carottes	un pamplemousse
du ketchup	une livre de beurre
des pommes	une salade
une sole	un kilo de pommes
un pot de confiture	de terre
un fromage	des cerises
un jambon	un yaourt
des sodas	une bouteille
un pain	d'eau minérale
de la limonade	un pot de mayonnaise
un paquet de café	des bananes
des haricots verts	un litre de lait
une boîte de céréales	une boîte de thon

REVIEW AND PRACTICE

CORRELATION: UNIT 3
(Theme: Food shopping)

Leçon 9   pp. T146-T153
Leçon 10   pp. T158-T161
Leçon 11   pp. T166-T167
Leçon 12   pp. T176-T177
see also: Visuals 27-33

a) Memory Game A: Students will look at the visual for a couple of minutes, and then in pairs (with the overhead projector turned off), list how many items they remember.

b) Memory Game B: Students will look at the visual for a couple of minutes, and then in pairs (with the overhead projector turned off), the teacher will name various items and the students will mark whether they were on the table or not.

c) Dialogue practice: One student will ask if his/her partner has purchased a given item, and the partner will respond, according to the transparency.
— Tu as acheté des poires?
— Non, mais j'ai acheté un kilo de bananes.

a) *Jeu de mémoire A: Regardez le dessin pendant une minute ou deux. Puis, avec un(e) camarade, faites la liste de toutes les choses que vous vous rappelez*

b) *Jeu de mémoire B: Regardez le dessin pendant une minute ou deux. Puis écoutez le professeur qui va mentionner différentes choses. Avec un(e) camarade, écrivez si oui ou non elles étaient sur la table.*

c) *Demandez à un(e) camarade si oui ou non il/elle a acheté certaines choses. Votre camarade répond en se basant sur le dessin.*

MEETING NATIONAL STANDARDS

GOAL 1:
COMMUNICATION

STANDARD 1.1
Interpersonal Communication: Engaging in conversation

With a partner, plan what you would like to serve for supper. How many of the ingredients have you already purchased (according to the visual)? What else will you need to buy?

Avec un(e) camarade, discutez ce que vous voulez servir pour le dîner. Selon le dessin, quels ingrédients avez-vous déjà achetés? Quelles autres choses avez-vous besoin d'acheter?

S9 Dans une boutique de disques

DESCRIPTION

Four photos of young people at a music store.

Note: The two young people that appear in the second photo from the top are named Karine and Sophie in the *Discovering French* text. If you wish, have students assign French names to the remaining young people in this transparency.

REVIEW AND PRACTICE

CORRELATION: UNIT 4
(theme: music and entertainment)

Reprise	p. T14
Leçon 5	p. T94
Leçon 13	pp. T193-T194
Leçon 15	pp. T212-T213
Leçon 16	pp. T222-T223
see also: **visual 35**	

MEETING NATIONAL STANDARDS

GOAL 1:
   COMMUNICATION

STANDARD 1.1
   Interpersonal Communication: Discussing preferences

Have pairs of students imagine conversations between two people in the visual.

Avec un(e) camarade, imaginez un dialogue entre deux personnes de la photo.

GOAL 1:
COMMUNICATION

STANDARD 1.3
Presentational Communication:
Describing preferences

Have students pick one of the people in the visual, and imagine what type of music he/she prefers and why? Describe the person's preferences, either orally or in writing.

Choisissez une personne de la photo, et imaginez quel genre de musique il/elle préfère. Dites pourquoi. Décrivez ses préférences, oralement ou par écrit.

S10 À Québec

DESCRIPTION

Five drawings of tourists in Quebec City superimposed on a street map of the city.

- **Au café (**in the background, the hotel **Château Frontenac)**
  Vous désirez?
  Apportez-moi…
- **Dans un taxi (**in the background, **à la porte Saint-Louis)**
  Connaissez-vous …?
- **Dans un restaurant (dans le quartier historique du "Vieux Québec")**
  Je vais prendre…
  Je voudrais…
- **À l'hôtel**
  Connaissez-vous…?
  Montrez-moi…
  Dites-moi comment aller…
- **À la terrasse d'un café, au Parc des Gouverneurs**
  Donnez-moi…

Note: If you wish, have students assign French names to the young people in this transparency.

REVIEW AND PRACTICE

CORRELATION: UNIT 4
(theme: Quebec)

Leçon 9   pp. T152-T153
Leçon 14   pp. T207; T209
Photo Essay 2   pp. T240-T247
see also: Visuals 2a, 2b

Read about Quebec, pp. 242-243.
Review verbs used to request services,
p. 226.

Révisez les verbes utilisés pour demander un service.

MEETING NATIONAL STANDARDS

GOAL 1:
COMMUNICATION

STANDARD 1.1
Interpersonal Communication:
Requesting services

Have pairs of students select one of the
scenes in the visual and invent an
appropriate dialogue.

Avec un(e) camarade, choisissez une des scènes du dessin et inventez un dialogue approprié.

MEETING NATIONAL STANDARDS

GOAL 1:
COMMUNICATION

STANDARD 1.3
Presentational Communication:
Presenting ideas

Have students pick one of the people in
the visual, and imagine that the person
is thinking aloud. What would he/she
be saying?

Choisissez une des personnes du dessin. Imaginez qu'il/elle pense tout haut (aloud). Qu'est-ce qu'il/elle dit?

DESCRIPTION

Five photos of young people engaged in sports.

le jogging	**faire du jogging, courir**
la natation	**nager**
le canoë (le bateau)	**faire du canoë, faire du bateau**
la planche à voile	**faire de la planche à voile**
le foot	**jouer au foot**

Note: If you wish, have students assign French names to the young people in this transparency.

REVIEW AND PRACTICE

CORRELATION: UNIT 5
(theme: sports and health)

Photo Essay 2	**pp. T86-T87**
Leçon 17	**pp. T254-T256**
Leçon 18	**p. T266; pp. T270-T271**
Leçon 25	**p. T347**
see also: **Visuals 40, 54**	

MEETING NATIONAL STANDARDS

GOAL 1:
COMMUNICATION

STANDARD 1.1
Interpersonal Communication:
Extending invitations

One student invites a classmate to join him/her in one of the sports shown in the Visual. The classmate politely declines, and suggests another sport (which could be one that is not shown). After some discussion, the two come to an agreement as to what they will do.

Invitez un(e) camarade à pratiquer avec vous un des sports montrés sur les photos. Votre camarade refuse poliment et suggère un autre sport (pas nécessairement montré sur les photos). Vous discutez, puis vous vous mettez d'accord (agree).

GOAL 1:

COMMUNICATION

STANDARD 1.3

Presentational Communication:
Presenting preferences

Pick one of the sports in the Visual and explain why you like it (or do not like it).

Choisissez un des sports montrés sur les photos et expliquez pourquoi vous aimez le pratiquer (ou non).

S12 Chez le médecin

DESCRIPTION

Drawing of the waiting room of Doctor Lebon's office. Six patients are sitting and agonizing as they await their turn.

Note: If you wish, have students assign French names to the people in this transparency.

Numéro 1 *(à gauche)* **a un rhume, un très mauvais rhume. Il a mal au nez.**

Numéro 2 a mal à la tête.

Numéro 3 a mal au pied.

Numéro 4 a mal au bras (au poignet: *wrist***).**

Numéro 5 a la grippe.

Numéro 6 a mal au ventre.

Another patient is talking to the receptionist.

Numéro 7 a mal à la main (au pouce: *thumb***).**

REVIEW AND PRACTICE

CORRELATION: UNIT 5
(theme: medical problems)

Leçon 17   p. T258; p. T260
Leçon 19   p. T274
Leçon 20   p. T289
see also: Visuals 41, 42

12 **Chez le médecin** (cont.)

MEETING NATIONAL STANDARDS

GOAL 1:
CCOMMUNICATION

STANDARD 1.1
Interpersonal Communication:
Explaining one's problems

Have pairs of students imagine
conversations between the doctor and
each of the patients.

*Avec un(e) camarade, imaginez un dialogue
entre le docteur et chacun des patients.*

MEETING NATIONAL STANDARDS

GOAL 1:
CCOMMUNICATION

STANDARD 1.1
Interpersonal Communication:
Discussing past events

Have pairs of students pick two of the
patients in the visual, and imagine a
conversation in which each one tells
what happened to cause his/her
medical problem.

*Avec un(e) camarade, choisissez deux des
patients du dessin. Chacun explique la
cause de son problème de santé. Jouez ce
dialogue.*

MEETING NATIONAL STANDARDS

GOAL 1:
CCOMMUNICATION

STANDARD 1.3
Presentational Communication:
Presenting ideas

Have students pick one of the people in
the visual, and imagine that the person
is thinking aloud. What would he/she
be saying?

*Choisissez une des personnes du dessin, et
imaginez qu'il/elle pense tout haut (aloud).
Qu'est-ce qu'il/elle dit?*

S13 La cuisine et le living

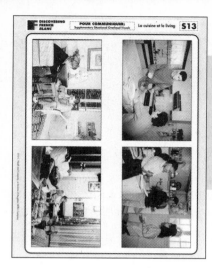

DESCRIPTION

Four photos: two kitchen scenes and two living room scenes.

Note: If you wish, have students assign French names to the young people in this transparency.

REVIEW AND PRACTICE

CORRELATION: UNIT 6
(theme: house and home)

Leçon 21   **pp. T298-T299;**
pp. T301-T303; p. T305
see also: **Visuals 20, 24, 47**

MEETING NATIONAL STANDARDS

GOAL 1:
COMMUNICATION

STANDARD 1.1
Interpersonal Communication:
Engaging in conversation

Have pairs of students imagine conversations between two people in the visual.

Avec un(e) camarade, imaginez un dialogue entre deux personnes de la photo.

MEETING NATIONAL STANDARDS

GOAL 1:
COMMUNICATION

STANDARD 1.1
Interpersonal Communication:
Making plans

Have pairs of students plan how they would remodel one of the rooms in the visual.

Avec un(e) camarade, dites comment vous voulez remodeler une des pièces sur les photos.

MEETING NATIONAL STANDARDS

GOAL 1:
COMMUNICATION

STANDARD 1.3
Presentational Communication:
Describing places

Have students describe both kitchens (or both living rooms) and then indicate which one they prefer and why.

Décrivez les deux cuisines (ou les deux livings), et dites laquelle (lequel) (which) vous préférez, et pourquoi.

DESCRIPTION

Three scenes from a robbery, accompanied by questions.

  A. (Two customers enter the bank)
   1. **Quelle heure était-il?**
   2. **Est-ce qu'il y avait beaucoup de clients dans la banque?**
   3. **Combien de personnes sont entrées?**
   4. **Comment était l'homme physiquement? Était-il grand ou petit? blond ou brun? Quel âge avait-il?**
   5.. **Quels vêtements portait-il?**
   6. **Décrivez l'aspect physique de la femme.**
   7. **Décrivez ses vêtements. Portait-elle une jupe longue ou courte?**

  B. (The bank teller hands over the money)
   8. **À qui est-ce que l'employé a donné l'argent?**
   9. **Qu'est-ce que l'homme a fait avec l'argent?**
   10. **Où est-ce que la femme a mis l'argent?**

  C. (The robbers flee the bank)
   11. **Quelle heure était-il quand les deux bandits sont sortis?**
   12. **Quel temps faisait-il?**
   13. **Est-ce qu'il y avait d'autres voitures dans la rue?**
   14. **Qu'est-ce que les bandits ont fait?**
   15. **Décrivez leur voiture.**

Note: If you wish, have students assign French names to the young people in this transparency.

Source: This transparency corresponds to Activité 9, Student Text, p. 333.

REVIEW AND PRACTICE

CORRELATION: UNIT 6
(theme: past narration)

Leçon 6   pp. T104-T107
Leçon 7   pp. T118-T119
Leçon 23   pp. T316-T322
Leçon 24   pp. T328-T333
see also: **Visuals 49, 51, 52**

Memory Game: The teacher will show the first scene for 30 seconds, then cover it and ask questions to see how well students remember what they saw.

Then the teacher will show the first scene so students can check the accuracy of what they remember.

Next the teacher shows them the second scene, etc.

Regardez le dessin pendant 30 seconds. Après, faites la liste de toutes les choses que vous vous rappelez.

MEETING NATIONAL STANDARDS

GOAL 1:
COMMUNICATION

STANDARD 1.1
Interpersonal Communication: Discussing past events

Students in pairs work together to continue the story, writing a conclusion. Who are the two bandits? Where do they go after the robbery? Are they caught? If so, how? If not, what happens to them?

Avec un(e) camarade, continuez l'histoire et dites comment elle a fini. Qui sont les deux bandits? Où vont-ils après le hold-up? Est-ce qu'ils sont pris? Si oui, comment? Sinon, qu'est-ce qui leur arrive?

S15 Au grand magasin

DESCRIPTION

Four photos of young people shopping for clothes.

Note: If you wish, have students assign French names to the young people in this transparency.

REVIEW AND PRACTICE

CORRELATION: UNIT 7
(theme: clothes and accessories)

Leçon 22	**p. T313**
Leçon 25	**pp. T344-T353**
Leçon 26	**pp. T356-T358; p. T360**
Leçon 27	**p. T368**
Leçon 28	**pp. T374-T376; pp. T378-T379**

see also: **Visuals 53-59**

MEETING NATIONAL STANDARDS

GOAL 1:
COMMUNICATION

STANDARD 1.1
Interpersonal Communication:
Engaging in conversation

Have pairs of students imagine conversations between two people in the visual.

Avec un(e) camarade, imaginez un dialogue entre deux personnes sur les photos.

DESCRIPTION

The top picture shows a bedroom scene before a burglary.

The bottom picture shows the same bedroom after the burglary.

Some of the things in the top scene have been taken, but others have either been left untouched, or knocked over and left on the floor.

REVIEW AND PRACTICE

CORRELATION: UNIT 7
(theme: clothes and accessories)

Leçon 25   pp. T346-T349
see also: **Visuals 53-56**

Review: pieces of furniture, Lesson 21, pp. 302-303.

• Show only the top picture, and have students describe the furniture and the things they see in the room.

Révisez le vocabulaire des meubles.

Décrivez les meubles et les objets que vous voyez dans la pièce.

MEETING NATIONAL STANDARDS

GOAL 1:
COMMUNICATION

STANDARD 1.3
Presentational Communication: Describing a scene

Have students write up a police report describing what the room looks like in the second scene.

Vous écrivez un rapport de police: décrivez l'aspect de la chambre dans la deuxième scène.

GOAL 1:
COMMUNICATION

STANDARD 1.3
Presentational Communication:
Narrating in the past

Have students use the the passé composé and the imperfect to narrate to a friend what happened last night. Which items were taken by the burglars **(les cambrioleurs)** and which items were moved or knocked over?

En utilisant le passé composé et l'imparfait, racontez à un(e) camarade ce qui est arrivé hier soir. Quels objets les cambrioleurs ont-ils pris? Quels objets ont changé de place ou ont été renversés (knocked over)?

S17   Jeunes touristes

DESCRIPTION

Photo of four young people tourists in a French train station.

Note: If you wish, have students assign French names to the young people in this transparency.

REVIEW AND PRACTICE

CORRELATION: UNIT 8
(theme: travel and summer vacation)

Leçon 5	pp. T98-T100
Leçon 7	p. T116
Leçon 29	pp. T402-T409
Leçon 30	pp. T412-T417
Leçon 31	pp. T420-T429
Leçon 32	p. T435

Photo Essays 1, 2, 3
see also: **Visuals 1, 1(o), 2a, 2b, 2c, 3, 4a, 4b, 5, 21-23, 60, 62, 64, 65**

MEETING NATIONAL STANDARDS

GOAL 1:
COMMUNICATION

STANDARD 1.1
Interpersonal Communication:
Engaging in conversation

Have students in groups of four act out the conversation among the young people in the photo.

Par groupes de quatre, jouez la conversation entre les jeunes de la photo.

MEETING NATIONAL STANDARDS

GOAL 1:
COMMUNICATION

STANDARD 1.3
Presentational Communication:
Describing people

Have students choose one of people in the picture, give that person a name and invent a personality. Then have them describe where that person is planning to go and what he/she wants to see and do.

Choisissez une des personnes de la photo. Donnez-lui un nom et une personnalité. Puis dites où il/elle veut aller et ce qu'il/elle veut voir et faire.

DESCRIPTION

Photo of lycée students sitting around a park after school. They are talking about their future plans, professions, where they will be living, etc.

Note: If you wish, have students assign French names to the people in this transparency.

REVIEW AND PRACTICE

CORRELATION: UNIT 8
(theme: clothes and accessories)

Leçon 1	**pp. T36-T37**
Leçon 4	**p. T66**
Leçon 21	**p. T300**
Leçon 31	**pp. T420-T421; p. T423**

see also: **Visuals 14, 15, 46, 50**

MEETING NATIONAL STANDARDS

GOAL 1:
COMMUNICATION

STANDARD 1.1
Interpersonal Communication:
Engaging in conversation

Have pairs of students imagine conversations between two people in the visual.

Avec un(e) camarade, imaginez un dialogue entre deux personnes de la photo.

DESCRIPTION

Photo of five young people around a new car.

Note: If you wish, have students assign French names to the young people in this transparency.

Source: Expansion of photo in Student Text, pp. 454-455.

REVIEW AND PRACTICE

CORRELATION: UNIT 9
  (theme: cars)

Leçon 27	**pp. T364-T365**
Unit 9 Opener	**pp. T454-T455**
Leçon 33	**pp. T456-T461**
see also: **visual 67**	

MEETING NATIONAL STANDARDS

GOAL 1:
  COMMUNICATION

STANDARD 1.1
  Interpersonal Communication: Engaging in conversation

Have pairs of students imagine conversations between two people in the visual; for instance, between one of owners of the new car and one of the friends who is admiring it.

Avec un(e) camarade, imaginez un dialogue entre deux personnes de la photo (par exemple entre un propriétaire de la voiture neuve, et une des personnes qui l'admirent).

GOAL 1:
COMMUNICATION

STANDARD 1.3
Presentational Communication:
Presenting ideas: role-play

Have students pick one of the people in the visual, and imagine that the person is thinking aloud. What would he/she be saying?

Choisissez une des personnes de la photo, et imaginez qu'il/elle pense tout haut (aloud). Qu'est-ce qu'il/elle dit?

S20 Leçon de conduite

DESCRIPTION

Cartoon depicting a driving lesson in which a highly erratic student driver has already caused several accidents to the great dismay of the driving teacher.

Note: If you wish, have students assign French names to the people in this transparency.

Source: Variation of cartoon in Student Text, p. 480.

REVIEW AND PRACTICE

CORRELATION: UNIT 9
(theme: getting around by car)

Leçon 33	**pp. T456-T461**
Leçon 34	**pp. T462-T466**
Leçon 36	**pp. T472-T475**

see also: **Visuals 66, 67**

MEETING NATIONAL STANDARDS

GOAL 1:
COMMUNICATION

STANDARD 1.1
Interpersonal Communication:
Engaging in conversation

Select one of the people in the cartoon and with a partner act out the conversation between this person and one of his/her family members at supper that night.

Choisissez une des personnes du dessin et, avec un(e) camarade, jouez le dialogue entre cette personne et un des membres de sa famille au dîner ce soir-là.

MEETING NATIONAL STANDARDS

GOAL 1:
COMMUNICATION

STANDARD 1.3
Presentational Communication:
Describing scenes

Describe the various accidents that the novice driver has caused.

Décrivez les divers accidents causés par le conducteur novice.

MEETING NATIONAL STANDARDS

GOAL 1:
COMMUNICATION

STANDARD 1.3
Presentational Communication:
Expressing emotions

Have students select one of the people in the cartoon, and imagine what he/she is saying or shouting.

Choisissez une des personnes du dessin, et imaginez ce qu'il/elle dit (ou crie!).

GOAL 1:

COMMUNICATION

STANDARD 1.3

Presentational Communication:
Making comparisons

Have students singly or in pairs compare this cartoon with the one in the Student Text, p. 480. Which one do they prefer and why?

Seul(e), ou avec un(e) camarade, comparez ce dessin avec celui de votre livre p. 480. Lequel préférez-vous? Pourquoi?

DESCRIPTION

Map of France with key cities and rivers.
On the overlay, the following are identified:

Cities (in bold face)

Lille	**Nantes**	**Nîmes**
Le Havre	**Tours**	**Avignon**
Caen	**Dijon**	**Nice**
Rouen	**Vichy**	**Cannes**
Versailles	**Annecy**	**Toulouse**
Paris	**Lyon**	**Montpellier**
Nancy	**Clermont-Ferrand**	**Marseille**
Strasbourg	**Grenoble**	**Toulon**
Rennes	**Bordeaux**	**Saint-Tropez**
Colmar	**Albi**	

Mountains (in capital letters)

les Vosges	**les Alpes**
le Massif Central	**les Pyrénées**

Rivers and bodies of water (in italics)

la Loire	**la Saône**	**l'Océan**
la Seine	**la Garonne**	**Atlantique**
la Meuse	**le Rhône**	**la Mer**
le Rhin	**la Manche**	**Méditerranée**

Neighboring countries (in capital letters)

l'Angleterre	**l'Allemagne**	**la Suisse**
la Belgique	**l'Espagne**	**l'Italie**
le Luxembourg	**Monaco**	

Source: Student text, Appendix, p. R15
Note: the transparency does not show the regions.

References and Activities in the Extended Teacher's Edition:
a) Lesson 2, p. T42
b) Lesson 4, p. T66
c) Photo Essay 1, p. T80
d) Lesson 8, p. T127

GOAL 3:
CONNECTIONS

STANDARD 3.1
Using French to further one's knowledge:
Geography

- Use the map and the overlay to help students learn to identify the physical features of France.
- Game: Devinez!
  One student thinks of a place named on the overlay and the others try to guess.

Un élève choisit un endroit sur la carte. Les autres élèves doivent deviner lequel (which).

[Vichy]
Est-ce que c'est une ville? [Oui.]
Est-ce que c'est Paris? [Oui.]
Est-ce que c'est au nord de Paris? [Non.] etc.

2a Le monde francophone

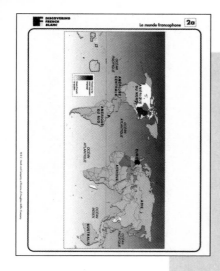

DESCRIPTION

Map of the world with French-speaking areas indicated in color.

Continents:
l'Amérique du Nord   l'Afrique
l'Amérique Centrale   l'Asie
l'Amérique du Sud   l'Australie
l'Europe

Oceans:
l'Océan Pacifique   l'Océan Indien
l'Océan Atlantique

Source: Student text, Appendix, pp. R16-R17 (without names of countries)

References and Activities in the Extended Teacher's Edition:
Use world map to locate francophone areas in conjunction with the following readings:
a) Photo Essay 1, p. T80
b) Photo Essay 2, p. T240
c) Photo Essay 3, p. T390

MEETING NATIONAL STANDARDS

GOAL 3:
CONNECTIONS

STANDARD 3.1
Using French to further one's knowledge:
Geography

- Make a large world map by projecting the Visual 2a on butcher paper which has been taped to the wall. Have the students trace the map onto the paper, and then identify the major countries in French.

- Assign each student a different French-speaking country, and have him/her consult a current almanac to find relevant information (e.g., capital city, population) which can be entered on the map.

*Calquez (trace) la carte sur le papier.
Identifiez les principaux pays en français.*

Le professeur vous a donné le nom d'un pays francophone. Dans un dictionnaire ou une encyclopédie, cherchez des renseignements (information) (capitale, population, etc.) que vous pouvez inscrire sur la carte.

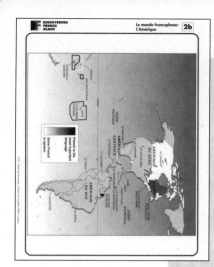

DESCRIPTION

Map of the North and South America and the South Pacific with French-speaking areas indicated in different shades showing:
- those places where French is the most important language, to
- those places where some French is spoken

French-speaking countries and areas:

l'Océan Pacifique:

la Nouvelle-Calédonie	**Tahiti**
la Polynésie française	**Wallis-et-Futuna**
Vanuatu	

l'Amérique du Nord:

Saint-Pierre-et-Miquelon	**le Québec**
la Nouvelle-Angleterre	**la Louisiane**

les Antilles *(no label):*

Haïti	**la Guadeloupe**	**la Martinique**

l'Amérique du Sud:
   la Guyane française

Other places:

l'Amérique du Nord

le Canada	**les États-Unis**

l'Amérique Centrale

le Mexique	**le Guatemala**
Cuba	**Porto Rico**

l'Amérique du Sud

	la Colombie
le Venezuela	**le Pérou**
le Brésil	**l'Argentine**

Source: Student text, Appendix, page R16.

Note: Student text does not label the "other places" listed above.

References and Activities in the Extended Teacher's Edition:

a) Lesson 1, p. T33	e) Lesson 29, p. T406
b) Lesson 15, p. T214	f) Lesson 30, p. T410
c) Photo Essay 2, p. T240	g) Lesson 30, p. T412
d) Lesson 27, p. T368	

MEETING NATIONAL STANDARDS

GOAL 3:
CONNECTIONS

STANDARD 3.1
Using French to further one's knowledge:
Current events

- Make and distribute copies of Visuals 2b and 2c to the students.

As an out-of-class project, have students collect newspaper or magazine clippings which refer to French-speaking countries, and identify these countries on their maps. A prize might be awarded to the student who finds references to the most countries.

Dans des journaux et des magazines, découpez (cut out) des articles sur des pays francophones. Identifiez ces pays sur les cartes. Vous gagnerez peut-être un prix!

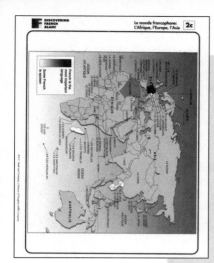

DESCRIPTION

Description: Map of the Asia, Europe and Africa with areas indicated in different shades showing:
- those places where French is the most important language
- those places where some French is spoken

French-speaking countries and areas:

Europe:

les îles Anglo-Normandes (Jersey, Guernsey)

la France	la Belgique
Monaco	le Luxembourg
Andorre	la Suisse
la Corse (France)	le Val d'Aoste (Italie)

Afrique:

le Maroc	la Guinée	la République
l'Algérie	le Burkina Faso	Centrafricaine
la Tunisie	le Côte d'Ivoire	le Congo
la Mauritanie	le Togo	le Zaïre
le Mali	le Bénin	le Rwanda
le Niger	Djibouti	le Burundi
le Tchad	le Cameroun	
le Sénégal	le Gabon	

l'Océan Indien:

les Seychelles	Madagascar	l'île Saint-Paul
les Comores	l'île Europe	les îles
Mayotte	l'île Bassas	Kerguelen
l'île Tromelin	da India	
l'île Maurice	les îles Crozet	
la Réunion	l'île Amsterdam	

l'Asie: Pondichéry

le Laos	le Cambodge	le Viêt-nam

Other countries:

La Norvège	Israël	la Corée du
La Suède	l'Égypte	Sud
Le Danemark	le Liban	le Japon
l'Allemagne	l'Inde	les Philippines
l'Irlande	La Russie	l'Indonésie
l'Angleterre	la Chine	l'Australie
le Portugal	la Corée du	
l'Espagne	Nord	
l'Italie		

Source: Student text, Appendix, page R17 *Note:* Student text does not label "other countries," listed above.

References and Activities in the
Extended Teacher's Edition:

a) Lesson 1, p. T33   e) Lesson 29, p. T406
b) Lesson 6, p. T104   f) Lesson 30, p. T410
c) Lesson 27, p. T368   g) Lesson 30, p. T412
d) Photo Essay 3, p. T390

 MEETING NATIONAL STANDARDS

GOAL 3:
CONNECTIONS

STANDARD 3.1
Using French to further one's knowledge:
Current events

Make and distribute copies of Visuals 2b and 2c to the students.
As an out-of-class project, have them collect newspaper or magazine clippings which refer to French-speaking countries, and identify these countries on their maps. A prize might be awarded to the student who finds references to the most countries.

Dans des journaux et des magazines, découpez des articles sur des pays francophones. Identifiez ces pays sur les cartes. Vous gagnerez peut-être un prix!

DESCRIPTION

Map of Europe with the following countries and places labelled:

l'Irlande	la Belgique
l'Angleterre	la France
le Luxembourg	l'Allemagne
Andorre	la Pologne
le Portugal	la Suisse
l'Espagne	l'Autriche
la Norvège	le Val d'Aoste
la Suède	Monaco
la Finlande	l'Italie
les Iles Anglo-Normandes	Grèce
le Danemark	la Corse
les Pays-Bas	la Russie

Océans	**Mer de Norvège**
Mer Noire	**Mer de Barents**

Overlay:

le Groenland	la Libye	Chypre
l'Islande	la République	le Liban
le Maroc	Tchèque	l'Iraq
la Sardaigne	la Slovaquie	Israël
les îles	la Hongrie	la Jordanie
Baléares	la Serbie	la Syrie
l'Algerie	la Yougoslavie	l'Estonie
la Sicile	la Macédoine	la Lettonie
la Tunisie	la Crète	la Lithuanie
la Slovénie	la Roumanie	la Biélorussie
la Croatie	la Bulgarie	l'Ukraine
la Bosnie	la Turquie	la Moldavie
l'Albanie		

Source: NEW ART

References and Activities in the Extended Teacher's Edition:
a) Lesson 1, p. T33
b) Photo Essay 1, p. T80

MEETING NATIONAL STANDARDS

GOAL 3:
CONNECTIONS

STANDARD 3.1
Using French to further one's knowledge:
Geography

Make and distribute copies of Visual 3 to the students.

Have them use an almanach or an atlas to find the names of all the countries and areas which are not identified. Then have them look up the French names of these places in a bilingual dictionary and enter them on the map (see Overlay Description for a list of these countries).

Cherchez dans une encyclopédie ou un atlas le nom de tous les pays ou autres endroits qui ne sont pas identifiés . Puis cherchez dans un dictionnaire bilingue le nom de ces endroits en français, et écrivez-le sur la carte.

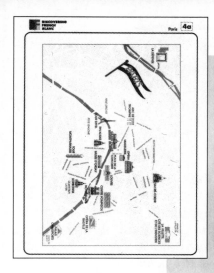

DESCRIPTION

Description: Map of Paris (and Nanterre) with selected monuments and streets.

Icons of monuments:
l'Arc de Triomphe
l'Opéra (Garnier)
l'Opéra de la Bastille
la Défense
le Louvre
la Sorbonne
la Tour Eiffel
la Tour Montparnasse
la Villette: Cité des Sciences et de l'Industrie
le Centre Pompidou
le Grand Palais
le Musée d'Orsay
le Palais Omnisports (Bercy)
les Invalides
Notre-Dame
la Place de la Concorde
le Sacré-Coeur

Sections of the city:
la Butte Montmartre	**le Quartier Latin**
la Rive Droite	**la Rive Gauche**

Source: NEW ART, cf. Student Text, p. 99.

References and Activities in the Extended Teacher's Edition:
a) Lesson 5, p. T99
b) Lesson 8, p. T128
c) Lesson 21, p. T305

★ MEETING NATIONAL STANDARDS

GOAL 3:
   CONNECTIONS

STANDARD 3.2
   Using French to find information:
   Internet

Have students use Internet to access Pariscope [http//:pariscope.fr] and find out additional information about one of the monuments or museums on the map: visiting days, hours, exhibits, other information.

Sur Internet, consultez Pariscope [http//:pariscope.fr] et cherchez des renseignements (information) *supplémentaires sur un des monuments ou des musées indiqués sur le plan: heures d'ouverture, expositions, etc...*

Note: Website addresses may sometimes change; some addresses may not be accessible, depending on your computer setup.

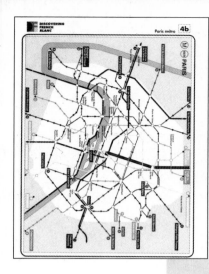

DESCRIPTION

Subway map of Paris with all main lines and certain stations labelled:

Main lines (end stations):

1. **Grande Arche de la Défense** — **Château de Vincennes**
2. **Porte Dauphine** — **Nation**
3. **Pont de Levallois–Bécon** — **Gallieni** (Gambetta, Porte des Lilas)
4. **Porte de Clignancourt** — **Porte d'Orléans**
5. **Bobigny–Pablo Picasso** — **Place d'Italie**
6. **Charles de Gaulle–Étoile** — **Nation**
7. **La Courneuve–8 mai 1945** (Louis Blanc, Pré St. Gervais) — **Villejuif–Louis Aragon**
8. **Balard** — **Créteil–Préfecture**
9. **Pont de Sèvres** — **Mairie de Montreuil**
10. **Boulogne–St Cloud** — **Gare d'Austerlitz**
11. **Châtelet** — **Mairie des Lilas**
12. **Mairie d'Issy** — **Porte de la Chapelle**
13. **Châtillon–Montrouge** — **St-Denis–Basilique, Gabriel Péri**

Additional métro stations:

Porte de la Villette	**Lamarck–Caulaincourt**
Place de Clichy	**Montparnasse–Bienvenüe**
Gare de l'Est	**Monceau**
Saint-Lazare	**Opéra**
République	**Franklin D. Roosevelt**
Madeleine	**La Motte-Picquet**
Concorde	**Palais-Royal**
Musée du Louvre	**Châtelet–Les Halles**
Hôtel de Ville	**Bastille**
Trocadéro	**Invalides**
Solférino	**Musée d'Orsay**
Denfert–Rochereau	**St-Michel**
Passy	**Champ de Mars–Tour Eiffel**
Cluny–la Sorbonne	**Cité**
Gare de Lyon	**Champs Élysées–**
Gare du Nord	**Clemenceau**

Source: NEW ART, cf. Student Text, p. 99

Note: the transparency map is more complete than the map on p. 99

References and Activities in the
Extended Teacher's Edition:
a) Lesson 5, p. T99
b) Lesson 21, p. T305

MEETING NATIONAL STANDARDS

GOAL 3:
CONNECTIONS

STANDARD 3.2
Using French to find information:
Internet

Copy Visual 4b and distribute it to the class. Have students in pairs use the Internet to access a complete subway map [http//paris.org.:/metro] and find out the names of all the subway stations on one of the 13 lines.

Sur Internet, avec un(e) camarade, consultez un plan détaillé du métro [http//paris.org.:/metro] et faites la liste des noms de tous les arrêts sur une des 13 lignes du métro.

Note: Website addresses may sometimes change; some addresses may not be accessible, depending on your computer setup.

GOAL 4:
COMPARISONS

STANDARD 4.2
Comparing English and French culture

Have students observe that some Paris subway stations are named after their location (e.g., Opéra, Tour Eiffel), some are named after people (e.g., de Gaulle, Roosevelt, Clemenceau), some are named after historical events such as battles (Austerlitz, Trocadéro, Solférino). [Encourage students to look up the names of the metro stations in the "culture section" at the back of the **Petit Larousse Illustré.**]

- What kinds of names are given to subway stops and/or bus stops in cities you are familiar with?
- How does the local system of naming stops compare with the French system?

Avez-vous remarqué que certains arrêts de métro à Paris sont nommés d'après (named after) leur emplacement (location) (Opéra, Tour Eiffel, par exemple), d'autres d'après des gens (par exemple De Gaulle, Roosevelt, Clemenceau) et d'autres d'après des événements historiques, des batailles par exemple (Austerlitz, Trocadéro, Solférino)?

- *Quel genre de noms ont les arrêts de métro et/ou d'autobus dans les villes que vous connaissez?*
- *Comparez le système d'appellation (naming) local avec le système français.*

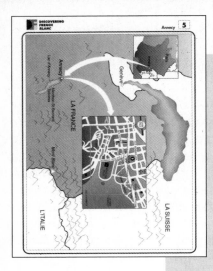

DESCRIPTION

Small map of France showing:
Paris, Annecy, Les Alpes

Large map of the Annecy region showing:
la Suisse, Genève (le Lac de Genève *not labelled*)
la France, Annecy, Menthon-St-Bernard,
Talloires, le Lac d'Annecy, le Mont-Blanc, l'Italie

Small street map of downtown Annecy showing:
Places:

Gare SNCF	**Champ de Mars**
Bonlieu	**Hotel de Vile**
(**"i"** *information*)	**Le Vieil Annecy**
"Le Garcin"	**Château**
Préfecture	**Lac d'Annecy**
Cité Administrative	

Streets and squares:

place de la Gare	**rue du Paquier**
rue Sommeiller	**place de la Libération**
place du Palais	**rue du Lac**
de Justice	**quai Eustache Chappuis**
rue Royale	

Source: NEW ART to show places where the video
program was filmed.

References and Activities in the
Extended Teacher's Edition:
a) Lesson 2, p. T42   c) Lesson 22, p. T307
b) Lesson 3, p. T54   d) Lesson 23, p. T314

MEETING NATIONAL STANDARDS

GOAL 3:
CONNECTIONS

STANDARD 3.2
Using French to find information:
Internet

- Have students use the Internet [http://www.calvacom.fr/relais/accueil.ht] to find out information about hotels in the Annecy area.

Sur Internet, renseignez-vous (get information) sur des hôtels de la région d'Annecy. [http://www.calvacom.fr/relais/accueil.ht]

- Have students use the Internet [http://web.urec.fr/france/france.html] to find out information about weather in the Annecy area.

Sur Internet, renseignez-vous sur le temps qu'il fait à Annecy. [http://web.urec.fr/france/france.html]

Note: Website addresses may sometimes change; some addresses may not be accessible, depending on your computer setup.

MEETING NATIONAL STANDARDS

GOAL 1:
COMMUNICATION

STANDARD 1.3
Presentational Communication:
Exchanging information

Have students prepare dialogues indicating where certain places are located.
— **Pardon, où est la gare SNCF?**
— **Elle est dans la rue Sommeiller.**
— **Est-ce que c'est loin? etc.**

Avec un(e) camarade, composez un dialogue pour indiquer où se trouvent certains endroits.

REVIEW AND PRACTICE
DF Bleu, UNITÉ 6

DESCRIPTION

Students studying the following subjects:

Marc	**le français**
Anne	**l'allemand**
Frédéric	**l'espagnol**
	l'histoire
	l'anglais
	la biologie (la bio)
Louise	**la chimie**
Jean	**la physique**
Louise et Jean	**les sciences**
Stéphanie	**les maths**
Jean-Philippe	**le dessin**
Corinne	**l'informatique**
	l'économie
Diane	**l'instruction civique**
Thomas	**la géographie (la géo)**
Éric	**l'éducation physique**

Source: NEW ART to illustrate vocabulary from Student
Text, p. 5

References and Activities in the
Extended Teacher's Edition:
a) Faisons connaissance!, p. T5
b) Rappel 3, p. T27
c) Lesson 6, p. T110

GOAL 4:
COMMUNICATION

STANDARD 4.1
Comparing English and French

Which names of school subjects are the same in the two languages?

Which school subjects are plural in English and singular in French?
[physics, economics]

Which are singular in English and plural in French?
[math, science]

Quelles matières scolaires ont le même nom dans les deux langues?

Quels noms de matières sont au pluriel en anglais et au singulier en français?

Et lesquels sont au singulier en anglais et au pluriel en français?

7   Quelques objets

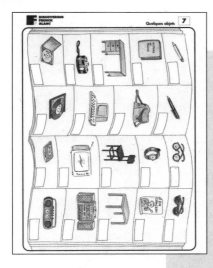

DESCRIPTION

Catalog pages with drawings of individual items. Next to each item is a box in which one can write a price.

un crayon	**une montre**
un livre	**une chaise**
un bureau	**une télé**
un appareil-photo	**une cassette**
un compact (disque)	**des lunettes de soleil**
un stylo	**une affiche**
un sac	**une table**
un ordinateur	**une chaîne-stéréo**
un disque	**une radiocassette**
des lunettes	

Source: NEW ART illustrating vocabulary from Student Text, p. R4

References and Activities in the Extended Teacher's Edition:
a) Rappel 1, p. T8   c) Lesson 6, p. T104
b) Rappel 2, p. T12   d) Lesson 27, p. T364

MEETING NATIONAL STANDARDS

GOAL 1:
COMMUNICATION

STANDARD 1.3
Presentational Communication:
Making oral presentations

Imagine it will soon be your birthday. Select one of the items shown and explain why you would like to receive it as a gift. Then select another item and explain why you would not like to have it as a gift.

Mon anniversaire, c'est samedi prochain. Comme cadeau, je voudrais avoir...

C'est bientôt votre anniversaire! Choisissez un des objets montrés dans le catalogue et expliquez pourquoi vous voudriez le recevoir en cadeau. Puis choisissez un autre objet et dites pourquoi vous ne voulez pas l'avoir en cadeau.

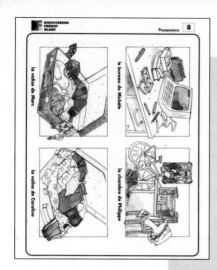

DESCRIPTION

Four pictures containing the following items:

- **le bureau de Michèle**

  un ordinateur   une radiocassette
  des livres   un stylo
  des cassettes   des crayons

- **la chambre de Philippe**

  une affiche   une table
  un vélo   un imperméable
    (une bicyclette)   (un imper)
  un sac   une chaise
  une chaîne-stéréo

- **la valise de Marc**

  une veste   un pantalon
  une cravate   un pull
  des chemises   des chaussettes

- **la valise de Caroline**

  un pull   un survêtement
  un chemisier   (un survêt)
  un maillot de bain   un jogging
  une jupe   une robe

Source: Student text, p. 13

*References and Activities in the
Extended Teacher's Edition:*
a) Rappel 2, p. T13   c) Lesson 2, p. T44
b) Rappel 2, p. T17   d) Lesson 28, p. 376

REVIEW AND PRACTICE

When students have reviewed the prepositions of place (Visual 10), have them practice describing the location of various objects.

— **Où est le livre rouge?**
— **Il est sur le bureau de Michèle (sous le livre jaune, à côté de l'ordinateur,...)**

Dites où sont différents objets.

MEETING NATIONAL STANDARDS

GOAL 4:
COMPARISONS

STANDARD 4.1
Comparing English and French

In casual French, words are often shortened by using only the first 1 or 2 syllables. What examples can you name?

[un imper, un survêt; also un pull(over), un vélo(cipède) la bio, la géo, les maths, la télé]

How are words shorted in English?

En français, dans la conversation, on raccourcit (shorten) souvent les mots à leur première syllabe, ou aux deux premières. Pouvez-vous donner des exemples?

Comment est-ce qu'on raccourcit les mots en anglais?

DESCRIPTION

Pictures of various places in or near a French town:

un café	un supermarché
un magasin de mode	un centre commercial
un hôtel	un stade
un cinéma (un ciné)	un musée
un restaurant	

une église	une maison
une école	une piscine
une bibliothèque	une plage
une boutique	

Source: NEW ART, illustrating vocabulary from Student Text, Appendix, p. R6

References and Activities in the Extended Teacher's Edition:
a) Rappel 2, p. T14
b) Lesson 18, p. T264
c) Lesson 36, p. T481

MEETING NATIONAL STANDARDS

GOAL 4:
COMPARISONS

STANDARD 4.1
Comparing English and French

- Which place names are similar in the two languages?

- Students can use French to expand their English vocabulary. Have them guess (or look up) the meanings of the following words by using as clues the related French terms:

powder magazine	**(magasin)**
ecclesiastical	**(église)**
scholarly	**(école)**

Perhaps students can discover other English words related to French.

- *Quels noms d'endroits sont les mêmes dans les deux langues?*

- *Vous pouvez utiliser le français pour enrichir votre vocabulaire anglais! Pouvez-vous deviner (sinon, chercher) le sens des mots suivants en pensant aux mots français qui leur ressemblent?*

bibliography	**(bibliothèque)**
pisciculture	**(piscine)**

Pouvez-vous trouver d'autres mots en anglais qui se ressemblent à leurs équivalents français?

10 Les prépositions

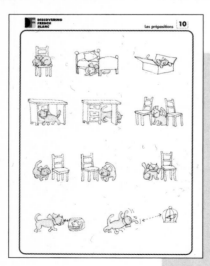

DESCRIPTION

Nine cat drawings illustrating the following prepositions:

sur la chaise	**à droite de** la chaise
sous le lit	**à côté de** la chaise
dans la boîte	**près du** poisson
devant le bureau	**(près du** bocal)
derrière le bureau	**loin de** l'oiseau
entre les chaises	**(loin de** la cage)
à gauche de la chaise	

Source: Art, Student Text, p. 15

References and Activities in the Extended Teacher's Edition:
a) Rappel 2, p. T15

When students have reviewed the prepositions of place, have them practice describing location by using Visual 8.

— **Où est le livre rouge?**
— **Il est sur le bureau de Michèle. (sous le livre jaune, à côté de l'ordinateur, …)**

Dites où sont les objets.

DESCRIPTION

The References and Activities in the house illustrate the following **-er** verbs:

habiter:	**Cette famille habite en France.**
regarder:	**Le chat sur le toit regarde les oiseaux.**
étudier:	**Le garçon étudie.**
préparer:	**Il prépare ses devoirs.**
téléphoner:	**La fille téléphone à un copain.**
parler:	**Elle parle avec son ami.**
organiser:	**Elle organise une boum.**
inviter:	**Elle invite ses copains.**
chanter:	**La jeune fille blonde chante.**
écouter:	**L'oiseau écoute la chanson. Il chante aussi.**
rentrer:	**Le père rentre à la maison. Le chie rentre avec lui.**
porter:	**Le père porte sa serviette** *(briefcase*
préparer:	**Dans la cuisine, la mère prépare l dîner.**
aider:	**Le petit frère aide sa mère.**
rester:	**Les deux jeunes restent au salon.**
regarder:	**Ils regardent la télé.**
jouer:	**À la télé, les hommes jouent au foo**
gagner:	**Qui va gagner le match?**
travailler:	**Le grand-père travaille dans le jardin.**
porter:	**Il porte un grand chapeau.**

Source: NEW ART; illustrating verbs from the Appendix, Student Text, pp. R8-R9

References and Activities in the Extended Teacher's Edition:
a) Rappel 3
b) Lesson 2, p. T44
c) Lesson 23, p. 316

Use this visual to review and practice furniture and the rooms of the house (Lesson 21).

MEETING NATIONAL STANDARDS

GOAL 1:
COMMUNICATION

STANDARD 1.1
Interpersonal Communication:
Engaging in conversation

Have pairs of students imagine conversations between two people in the visual.

Avec un(e) camarade, composez un dialogue entre deux personnes sur le dessin.

MEETING NATIONAL STANDARDS

GOAL 1:
COMMUNICATION

STANDARD 1.3
Presentational Communication:
Presenting ideas

Have students pick one of the people in the visual, and imagine that the person is thinking aloud. What would he/she be saying?

Choisissez une des personnes du dessin, et imaginez qu'il/elle pense tout haut (out loud). Qu'est-ce qu'il/elle dit?

DESCRIPTION

The References and Activities in the street **(en ville)** illustrate the following **-er** verbs:

acheter:	**La jeune fille achète un magazine.**
regarder:	**Le garçon regarde un journal.**
marcher:	**Les trois copains marchent dans la rue.**
écouter:	**Le garçon écoute son walkman.**
apporter:	**Au café, le serveur apporte une limonade et un café.**
parler:	**Au café, il y a un garçon qui parle anglais.**
rencontrer:	**Les jeunes rencontrent leurs amis au café.**

The activities at the party **(à la boum)** illustrate the following **-er** verbs:

manger:	**Les jeunes au buffet mangent des sandwiches.**
danser:	**Trois jeunes dansent. Ils aiment danser.**
apporter:	**Le garçon à droite apporte un nouveau compact.**

Source; NEW ART; illustrating verbs from the Appendix, Student Text, pp. R8-R9.

References and Activities in the Extended Teacher's Edition:
a) Rappel 3
b) Lesson 2, p. T44
c) Lesson 23, p. 316

MEETING NATIONAL STANDARDS

GOAL 1:
COMMUNICATION

STANDARD 1.1
Interpersonal Communication:
Engaging in conversation

Have pairs of students imagine
conversations between two people in
the visual.

*Avec un(e) camarade, composez un
dialogue entre deux personnes sur
le dessin.*

MEETING NATIONAL STANDARDS

GOAL 1:
COMMUNICATION

STANDARD 1.3
Presentational Communication:
Presenting ideas

Have students pick one of the people in
the visual, and imagine that the person
is thinking aloud. What would he/she
be saying?

*Choisissez une des personnes du dessin,
et imaginez qu'il/elle pense tout haut
(out loud). Qu'est-ce qu'il/elle dit?*

DESCRIPTION

The References and Activities in the four pictures illustrate the following **-ir** verbs:

réussir à un examen: Marc réussit à son examen.

maigrir: Qui veut maigrir?

grossir: Qui veut grossir?

choisir: La jeune fille choisit un tee-shirt.

réussir: Marc a réussi.
[Il va devenir chirurgien.]

finir: La jeune fille finit la course. Elle arrive première.

Source: NEW ART; illistrating verbs from the Appendix, Student Text, p. R11.

References and Activities in the Extended Teacher's Edition:
a) Rappel 3, p. T22
b) Lesson 23, p. T316

MEETING NATIONAL STANDARDS

GOAL 1:
COMMUNICATION

STANDARD 1.1
Interpersonal Communication: Engaging in conversation

Have pairs of students imagine conversations between two people in the visual.

Avec un(e) camarade, composez un dialogue entre deux personnes sur le dessin.

MEETING NATIONAL STANDARDS

GOAL 1:
COMMUNICATION

STANDARD 1.3
Presentational Communication:
Presenting ideas

Have students pick one of the people in the visual, and imagine that the person is thinking aloud. What would he/she be saying?

Choisissez une des personnes du dessin, et imaginez qu'il/elle pense tout haut. Qu'est-ce qu'il/elle dit?

12b Quelques activités: Les verbes en *-re*

DESCRIPTION

The References and Activities in the three pictures illustrate the following -re verbs:

à dix heures et demie
répondre: La jeune fille répond à la question.
Elle répond au professeur.

à quatre heures et demie
perdre: La jeune fille perd son livre.
entendre: Le monsieur n'aime pas entendre la musique moderne.
attendre: Le garçon au café attend son copain.

à cinq heures et demie
rendre visite à: La jeune fille va rendre visite à sa grand-mère.
vendre: Le monsieur lui vend des fleurs.

Source: NEW ART; illustrating verbs from the Appendix, Student Text, p. R11.

References and Activities in the Extended Teacher's Edition:
a) Rappel 3, p. T22   b) Lesson 23, p. T316

MEETING NATIONAL STANDARDS

GOAL 1:
COMMUNICATION

STANDARD 1.1
Interpersonal Communication:
Engaging in conversation

Have pairs of students imagine conversations between two people in the visual.

Avec un(e) camarade, composez un dialogue entre deux personnes sur le dessin.

MEETING NATIONAL STANDARDS

GOAL 1:
COMMUNICATION

STANDARD 1.3
Presentational Communication:
Presenting ideas

Have students pick one of the people in the visual, and imagine that the person is thinking aloud. What would he/she be saying?

Choisissez une des personnes du dessin, et imaginez qu'il/elle pense tout haut. Qu'est-ce qu'il/elle dit?

MEETING NATIONAL STANDARDS

GOAL 4:
COMPARISONS

STANDARD 4.1
Comparing English and French

Sometimes words in English and French look the same but have different meanings.

- What are these pairs of words called? [false cognates]
- What is an example of a false cognate in this visual? [**attendre**, which does not mean "to attend" but "to wait" or "to wait for."]
- Can you think of other false cognates? [e.g., **assister à**, "to attend," not "to help or assist"; etc.]

Quelquefois des mots français et anglais se ressemblent, mais ils n'ont pas le même sens.

- *Comment s'appellent ces mots?*

- *Pouvez-vous donner un exemple de faux amis sur ce dessin?*

- *Pouvez-vous penser à d'autres faux amis?*

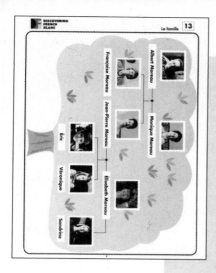

DESCRIPTION

This family tree illustrates the following vocabulary:

le grand-père, la grand-mère
le mari, la femme
le père, la mère
le beau-père, la belle-mère
la tante
le frère, la soeur
le demi-frère, la demi-soeur
le neveu, la nièce
le petit-fils, la petite-fille
les parents, les enfants
les grands-parents, les petits-enfants

Additional vocabulary:
l'oncle; la belle-fille

Source: Student Text, Activité 5, p. 35

References and Activities in the
Extended Teacher's Edition:
a) Lesson 1, Activité 5, p. 35
   Once students have done the first part of Activité 5, this
   transparency can be shown to let them check their work.
b) Lesson 15, p. T216

REVIEW AND PRACTICE

Use Visual 13 to practice and review possessive adjectives, e.g.,

Voici Véronique. **Son** frère s'appelle Éric. **Sa** demi-soeur s'appelle Sandrine.
Albert et Monique Moreau parlent: "Françoise et Jean-Pierre sont **nos** enfants."

MEETING NATIONAL STANDARDS

GOAL 1:
COMMUNICATION

STANDARD 1.3
Presentational Communication:
Introducing people

Have students each pick one of the people in the visual, and introduce that person to the class. Where does the person live? What does he/she like to do? etc.

Choisissez une des personnes du dessin, et présentez-le/la à la classe. Où habite-t-il/elle? Qu'est-ce qu'il/elle aime faire? etc.

MEETING NATIONAL STANDARDS

GOAL 4:
COMPARISONS

STANDARD 4.1
Comparing English and French

Compare the English and French forms of the following terms:

grandfather   le **grand**-père
grandmother   la **grand**-mère
grandparents   les **grands**-parents

Which naming system seems more logical?

Comparez les mots suivants en français et en anglais.

grandson   le **petit**-fils
granddaughter   la **petite**-fille
grandchildren   les **petits**-enfants

Quel système vous semble le plus logique?

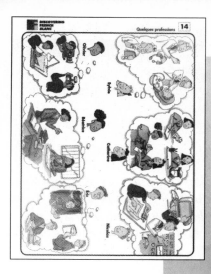

DESCRIPTION

Six young people are considering various professions:

- **Sylvie** — **médecin, dentiste, infirmière**
- **Catherine** — **comptable, employée de bureau, vendeuse**
- **Nicolas** — **informaticien, technicien, ingénieur**
- **Olivier** — **cinéaste, photographe, dessinateur**
- **Béatrice** — **femme d'affaires/patronne, avocate**
- **Éric** — **acteur, journaliste, écrivain**

Source: NEW ART illustrating vocabulary of Student Text, p. 37

References and Activities in the Extended Teacher's Edition:
a) Lesson 1, p. T37
b) Lesson 31, p. T423

REVIEW AND PRACTICE

- Review the school subjects in Visual 6. What subjects are the students in Visual 14 studying? What are their favorite subjects? What subjects do they not like?

- Review the descriptive adjectives in Visual 15. Use these adjectives to describe the people in Visual 14.

- *Révisez les matières de l'image 6. Quelles matières est-ce que les élèves de l'image 14 étudient? Quelles sont leurs matières préférées? Quelles matières est-ce qu'ils n'aiment pas?*

- *Choisissez une des personnes du dessin et présentez-le/la à la classe. Quel âge a-t-il/elle? À quoi est-ce qu'il/elle s'intéresse? Qu'est-ce qu'il/elle veut faire plus tard?*

MEETING NATIONAL STANDARDS

GOAL 1:

COMMUNICATION

STANDARD 1.3

Presentational Communication:
Introducing people

Have students each pick one of the people in the visual, and introduce that person to the class. How old is the person? What are his/her interests? What does he/she want to do in the future?

Choisissez une des personnes du dessin et présentez-le/la à la classe. Quel âge a-t-il/elle? À quoi est-ce qu'il/elle s'intéresse? Qu'est-ce qu'il/elle veut faire plus tard?

DESCRIPTION

Street scene which can be used to present descriptive adjectives, for example:

• **Mlle Martin**	**jeune, sportive, active, belle**
• **M. Duval**	**vieux, sportif, actif, heureux, aimable**
• **Éric**	**jeune, grand, sympa(thique), beau**
• **Philippe**	**sérieux, intellectuel, ambitieux**
• **Isabelle**	**triste, timide, mignonne**
• **Malice**	**amusant, drôle, bête, impulsif**
• **Henri**	**jeune, petit, curieux, mignon**
• **Mme Camus**	**grande, contente, heureuse**
la voiture Toyota	**grande, jolie, vieille, bonne, japonaise**
le vélo Peugeot	**nouveau, beau, français**
la bicyclette Peugeot	**nouvelle, belle, française**
le scooter Motobécane	**grand, joli, beau, français**

Source: NEW ART illustrating selected adjectives, Student Text, pp. 46-48

References and Activities in the Extended Teacher's Edition:
a) Lesson 2, p. T50

REVIEW AND PRACTICE

Descriptions of Visual 15 can also be used to practice **c'est/il est**:

Regardez cette voiture. **C'est** une Toyota. Elle est japonaise. **C'est** une bonne voiture.

MEETING NATIONAL STANDARDS

GOAL 1:
COMMUNICATION

STANDARD 1.2
Interpretive Communication:
Understanding spoken language

Invent interior monologues for people on the visual and speak these aloud to the class. The students practice their listening skills as they try and guess whose thoughts your are expressing.

E.g., **Oh, regarde le petit chien. J'adore les chiens! Est-ce qu'il va venir me dire bonjour? [Henri]**

Le professeur va (Je vais) dire tout haut ce que pense une des personnes sur le dessin. Écoutez bien! Pouvez-vous deviner qui parle?

MEETING NATIONAL STANDARDS

GOAL 4:
COMPARISONS

STANDARD 4.1
Comparing English and French

How do the French express the sound of a motor scooter? **[Pof]**

What expression would one use in English? **[Putt-putt]**

Which language comes closest, in your opinion, to the sound of a scooter?

Do you remember other French expressions for sounds? [From *DF-Bleu*, Unit 2]

tic-tac (tick tock)
toc! toc! (knock, knock)
drin... drin... (ding-a-ling)
boum! (boom)
din don (ding dong)
ploc... ploc... (splish splash)

Comment exprime-t-on en français le bruit d'un moteur de scooter?

Et en anglais?

À votre avis, quelle langue exprime le mieux le bruit d'un scooter?

Connaissez-vous d'autres expressions françaises pour d'autres bruits?

DESCRIPTION

Eight drawings illustrate expressions with **avoir**.

- **Simon**   **Il a faim.** (C'est un chimpanzé.)
- **Philippe**   **Il a chaud.** (Il se trouve au désert.)
- **Alice**   **Elle a peur.** (Elle fait un tour sur les Montagnes Russes.)
- **Henri**   **Il a tort.** (Il ne saît pas la bonne réponse.)
- **Jacques**   **Il a sommeil.** (Il dort en classe.)
- **Mlle Dumas**   **Elle a de la chance.** (Elle gagne toujours à la roulette.)
- **M. Mercier**   **Il a froid.** (Il n'a pas d'anorak.)
- **Louise**   **Elle a soif.** (Elle boit de l'eau minérale.)

Source: NEW ART to illustrate vocabulary in Student Text, p. 56.

References and Activities in the Extended Teacher's Edition:
a) Lesson 3, p. T56

REVIEW AND PRACTICE

Use Visual 16 for a rapid-fire drill of **avoir** expressions.

E.g., **Maintenant** *[pointing to Jacques]* **... il a sommeil.**
    [pointing to Louise] **... elle a soif, etc.**
    Hier aussi *[pointing to Philippe]* **... il a eu chaud, etc.**

De temps en temps, moi *[pointing to Alice]* **... j'ai peur, etc.**
En ce moment, nous *[indicating negation, pointing to Simon]* **... nous n'avons pas faim, etc.**

MEETING NATIONAL STANDARDS

GOAL 1:
COMMUNICATION

STANDARD 1.3
Presentational Communication:
Narrating past events

Have students pick one of the people in the visual describe what happened, using their imagination. (This activity works best in conjunction with Unité 6.)

Choisissez une personne (ou le chimpanzé!) sur les dessins, et dites ce qui s'est passé. Utilisez votre imagination!

MEETING NATIONAL STANDARDS

GOAL 4:
COMPARISONS

STANDARD 4.1
Comparing English and French

What is the general meaning of **avoir** in a sentence like: **J'ai un chien**?

What is the English equivalent of each of the **avoir** expressions illustrated in the Visual 16? Does English also use the verb "to have"?

Which expression in each pair seems to be the most expressive:

Quel est le sens général de avoir dans une phrase comme: J'ai un chien?

Quel est l'équivalent en anglais de chacune des expressions avec avoir illustrées dans ces dessins? Est-ce qu'on utilise aussi le verbe "to have" en anglais?

Quelle expression de chaque paire vous semble la plus expressive?

I have hunger.	I am hungry.
We have fear.	We are afraid.
She has luck.	She is lucky.
He has sleep.	He is sleepy.
They have heat.	They are hot.
You have reason.	You are right.

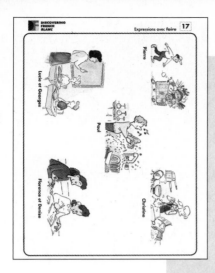

DESCRIPTION

Five drawings illustrate expressions with **faire**:

- **Pierre**   Il fait les courses.
- **Christine**   Elle fait la cuisine.
- **Paul**   Il fait la vaisselle.
- **Lucie et Georges** Ils font attention.
                        Est-ce qu'ils font de l'anglais?
- **Florence et Denise** Elles font leurs devoirs.
                        Est-ce qu'elles font des maths?

Source: Art adapted to illustrate vocabulary in Student Text, p. 58

References and Activities in the Extended Teacher's Edition:
a) Lesson 3, p. T58
b) Lesson 36, p. T480

REVIEW AND PRACTICE

Use Visual 17 for a rapid-fire drill of **faire** expressions.

E.g., **Maintenant** *[pointing to Pierre]* ... il fait les courses.
[pointing to Christine] ... elle fait la cuisine, etc.
Hier aussi *[pointing to Paul]* ... il a fait la vaisselle, etc.

Généralement, moi *[pointing to Lucie and Georges]* ... je fais attention, etc.
En ce moment, nous *[indicating negation, pointing to Florence et Denise]* ... nous ne faisons pas nos devoirs, etc.

GOAL 4:
COMPARISONS

STANDARD 4.1
Comparing English and French

What is the general meaning of **faire** in a sentence like: **Qu'est-ce que tu fais?**

What is the English equivalent of each of the **faire** expressions illustrated in the Visual 17? In which ones does English also use the verb "do"? What about the others?

Is it always possible to give word-for-word translations from English to French? Why not?

Quel est le sens général de faire dans une phrase comme: Qu'est-ce que tu fais?

Quel est l'équivalent en anglais de chacune des expressions avec faire illustrées dans ces dessins? Dans quelles expressions utilise-t-on aussi le verbe "to do" en anglais? Et pour les autres expressions, qu'est-ce qu'on dit?

Est-il toujours possible de traduire (translate) *mot à mot de l'anglais au français? Pourquoi pas?*

18   Où vont-ils? D'où viennent-ils?

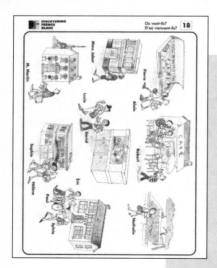

DESCRIPTION

Eight scenes illustrating **aller** and **venir**.

Pierre et Alain vont au stade.
Robert va au café.
Nathalie vient de la piscine.
Madame Jabot va au Bureau de tourisme.
Lucie et Robert viennent du cinéma.
M. Martin va à Paris. Il va à l'hôtel.
Sophie et Hélène viennent de la bibliothèque.
Éric, Paul et Sylvie viennent de l'école.

Source: NEW ART, verbs reviewed in Student Text, p. 66, p. 68

References and Activities in the Extended Teacher's Edition:
a) Lesson 4, p. T68
b) Lesson 7, p. T119
c) Lesson 16, p. T230

REVIEW AND PRACTICE

Use Visual 18 with Lesson 18 to practice the pronouns **y** and **en**.

Est-ce que Pierre va **au stade?**
Oui, il **y** va.
Est-ce que David va **au ciné?**
Non, il n'**y** va pas. Il **en** vient.

MEETING NATIONAL STANDARDS

GOAL 1:
COMMUNICATION

STANDARD 1.1
Interpersonal Communication:
Engaging in conversation

Have pairs of students imagine conversations between two people in the visual.

Avec un(e) camarade, composez un dialogue entre deux personnes sur le dessin.

MEETING NATIONAL STANDARDS

GOAL 1:
COMMUNICATION

STANDARD 1.3
Presentational Communication:
Presenting ideas

Have students pick one of the people in the visual, and imagine that the person is thinking aloud. What would he/she be saying?

Choisissez une des personnes du dessin, et imaginez qu'il/elle pense tout haut. Qu'est-ce qu'il/elle dit?

ACTIVITIES • A77

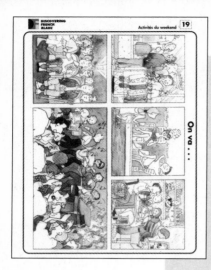

DESCRIPTION

Five scenes showing weekend activities:

Ils vont en ville.	**Ils vont aller dans les magasins.** **Ils vont faire des achats.**
Ils vont à la piscine.	**Ils vont bronzer.** **Ils vont prendre un bain de soleil.**
Ils vont au café.	**Ils vont rencontrer des copains.** **Ils vont retrouver des amis.** **Ils vont jouer au flipper.**
Ils vont au ciné.	**Ils vont voir un film.**
Ils vont au théâtre (au stade).	**Ils vont assister à un concert de rock.** **(Ils vont sortir avec des copains.)**

Source: NEW ART to illustrate vocabulary in Student Text, p. 96.

References and Activities in the Extended Teacher's Edition:
a) Lesson 5, p. T96
b) Lesson 8, p. T130
c) Lesson 23, p. T316

REVIEW AND PRACTICE

Use Visual 19 with Lesson 18 to
practice the pronoun **y**.

[point to upper left picture]

Est-ce que les jeunes sont à la campagne?
Non, ils n'**y** sont pas. Ils sont en ville.

MEETING NATIONAL STANDARDS

GOAL 1:
COMMUNICATION

STANDARD 1.1
Interpersonal Communication:
Engaging in conversation

Have pairs of students imagine
conversations between two people in
the visual.

*Avec un(e) camarade, composez un
dialogue entre deux personnes sur le
dessin.*

MEETING NATIONAL STANDARDS

GOAL 1:
COMMUNICATION

STANDARD 1.3
Presentational Communication:
Presenting ideas

Have students pick one of the people in
the visual, and imagine that the person
is thinking aloud. What would he/she
be saying?

*Choisissez une des personnes du dessin, et
imaginez qu'il/elle pense tout haut. Qu'est-
ce qu'il/elle dit?*

D E S C R I P T I O N

Scene illustrating various weekend activities around the house:

Les enfants restent à la maison aujourd'hui.
- **[Vincent] range sa chambre. Il range ses affaires.**
- **[Claire] nettoie sa chambre.**
- **[Thomas et Annick] aident leurs parents. Ils font la vaisselle.**
- **[Sylvie] nettoie le garage.**
- **[Mathieu et Michel] lavent la voiture.**

Source: NEW ART to illustrate vocabulary in Student Text, p. 96.

References and Activities in the Extended Teacher's Edition:
a) Lesson 5, p. T96
b) Lesson 8, p. T130
c) Lesson 23, p. T316

M E E T I N G   N A T I O N A L   S T A N D A R D S

GOAL 1:
COMMUNICATION

STANDARD 1.3
Presentational Communication:
Writing about past events

Have students pick one of the people in the visual, and imagine that the person is writing a diary entry about the day's events. In the morning he/she had to help around the house (describe the chores). In the afternoon, he/she was free to go out. Imagine what he/she did.

Choisissez une des personnes du dessin. Il/elle écrit dans son journal ce qu'il/elle a fait aujourd'hui. Le matin il/elle a dû aider à la maison (décrivez). L'après-midi il/elle a pu sortir. Imaginez ce qu'il/elle a fait.

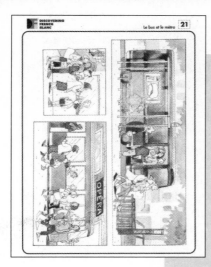

DESCRIPTION

Paris street scenes illustrating the following vocabulary:

Comment vas-tu aller au concert?
 Je vais **marcher.**
 Je vais **aller à pied.**
 Je vais **prendre le bus.**
 Je vais **prendre le métro.**

Dans le métro:
 Je vais acheter **un billet de métro (un ticket de métro).**
 Je vais **monter** à Opéra.
 Ils vont **descendre** à Opéra.

Source: NEW ART to illustrate vocabulary in Student Text, p. 98.

References and Activities in the Extended Teacher's Edition:
a) Lesson 5, p. T98

REVIEW AND PRACTICE

Follow up this activity by using Visual 4b to plan subway trips from one point to the other in Paris.

MEETING NATIONAL STANDARDS

GOAL 1:
COMMUNICATION

STANDARD 1.1
Interpersonal Communication:
Engaging in conversation

Have pairs of students imagine
conversations between two people in
the visual.

*Avec un(e) camarade, composez un
dialogue entre deux personnes sur le
dessin.*

MEETING NATIONAL STANDARDS

GOAL 1:
COMMUNICATION

STANDARD 1.3
Presentational Communication:
Presenting ideas

Have students pick one of the people in
the visual, and imagine that the person
is thinking aloud. What would he/she
be saying?

*Choisissez une des personnes du dessin, et
imaginez qu'il/elle pense tout haut. Qu'est-
ce qu'il/elle dit?*

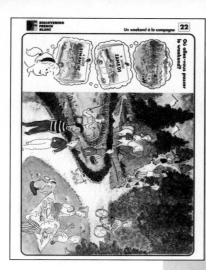

DESCRIPTION

Two scenes showing the following activities:

Sylvie pense...
  Nous allons passer le weekend à la campagne.
  Nous allons partir samedi matin.
  Nous allons rentrer dimanche soir.

À la campagne, on peut...
  faire une randonnée
  faire une promenade à cheval
  faire un tour à vélo
  aller à la pêche
  faire un pique-nique
  faire une promenade à pied

Source: NEW ART to illustrate vocabulary in Student Text, p. 100.

References and Activities in the
Extended Teacher's Edition:
a) Lesson 5, p. T100

REVIEW AND PRACTICE

Use Visual 22 to review and practice the use of the imperfect to describe habitual past actions. Describe what the people in the visual used to do when they were on vacation.

Dites ce que les personnes sur le dessin faisaient quand elles étaient en vacances.

MEETING NATIONAL STANDARDS

GOAL 1:
COMMUNICATION

STANDARD 1.1
Interpersonal Communication:
Engaging in Conversation

Have pairs of students imagine conversations between two people in the visual.

Avec un(e) camarade, composez un dialogue entre deux personnes sur le dessin.

MEETING NATIONAL STANDARDS

GOAL 1:
COMMUNICATION

STANDARD 1.3
Presentational Communication:
Presenting ideas

Have students pick one of the people in the visual, and imagine that the person is thinking aloud about his/her weekend plans. Where will he/she go? With whom? What will they do Saturday morning? Saturday afternoon? Sunday afternoon?

Choisissez une des personnes du dessin, et imaginez qu'il/elle pense tout haut à ce qu'il/elle va faire ce weekend. Où va-t-il/elle aller? avec qui? Qu'est-ce qu'ils/elles vont faire le samedi matin? le samedi après-midi? le dimanche après-midi?

23 À la campagne

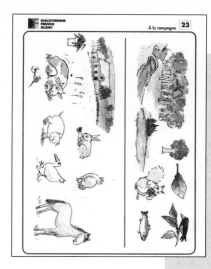

DESCRIPTION

Spot art depicting the following vocabulary:

une forêt	un oiseau	un écureuil
un arbre	une rivière	un poisson
une feuille	un lac	

une ferme	une plante	un canard
un champ	une vache	un cheval
un lapin	une fleur	
une poule	un cochon	

Source: illustrations from Student Text, p. 100.

References and Activities in the Extended Teacher's Edition:
a) Lesson 5, p. T100
b) Lesson 7, p. T219

MEETING NATIONAL STANDARDS

GOAL 4:
COMPARISONS

STANDARD 4.1
Comparing English and French

Review French animal sounds from *DF-Bleu*, Unit 2, and compare these to the English versions. Which seem to be more "accurate"?

	la vache: **meuh**
	la poule: **cot...cot...codèt**
Also:	le cheval: **hi...hi...hi**

Dans DF Bleu, Unité 2, révisez les cris des animaux. Comparez-les à leur équivalent en anglais. Dans quelle langue vous semblent-ils le plus "exacts"?

le canard: **coin coin**

le cochon: **oink-oink**
[pronounced: /waɛ̃k-waɛ̃k/]

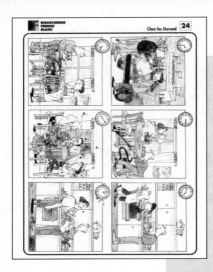

DESCRIPTION

Series of six pictures showing a sequence of activities which can be narrated using adverbs of time.

Samedi dernier, Georges et Delphine ont invité leurs amis à dîner.

À deux heures et demie…　　**Avant,** ils ont fait les course

À trois heures et quart…　　**D'abord,** ils ont nettoyé la maison.

À cinq heures moins le quart…　　**Ensuite,** ils ont fait la cuisin

À cinq heures vingt…　　**Finalement,** ils ont mis la table.

À huit heures dix…　　**Enfin,** ils ont dîné avec leur invités.

　　Pendant le repas, ils ont écouté de la musique.

À une heure du matin…　　**Après,** ils ont fait la vaissell

Source: NEW ART to illustrate vocabulary in Student Text, p. 106.

References and Activities in the Extended Teacher's Edition:
a) Lesson 6, p. T106
b) Lesson 15, p. T219

MEETING NATIONAL STANDARDS

GOAL 1:
COMMUNICATION

STANDARD 1.1
Interpersonal Communication:
Engaging in phone conversations

Students imagine that Madame Durand is phoning a friend the next day and is talking about the dinner party. The friend has a lot of questions. Have students play the roles of Mme Durand and her friend.

Madame Durand téléphone à un(e) ami(e) le lendemain, et raconte le dîner. L'ami(e) pose beaucoup de questions. Avec un(e) camarade, jouez ce dialogue.

MEETING NATIONAL STANDARDS

GOAL 1:
COMMUNICATION

STANDARD 1.3
Presentational Communication:
Presenting ideas

Have students pick one of the people in the visual, and imagine that the person is thinking aloud. What would he/she be saying?

Choisissez une des personnes du dessin, et imaginez qu'il/elle pense tout haut. Qu'est-ce qu'il/elle dit?

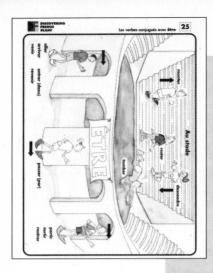

DESCRIPTION

References and Activities in the "**être**" stadium help students remember which verbs are conjugated with **être** in the passé composé.

monter	arriver	passer (par)
descendre	venir	partir
rester	entrer (dans)	sortir
tomber	revenir	rentrer
aller		

Source: NEW ART to illustrate vocabulary in Student Text, p. 128.
[All **être** verbs from the text are shown except **devenir**.]

References and Activities in the Extended Teacher's Edition:
a) Lesson 8, p. T128

REVIEW AND PRACTICE

Use Visual 25 for rapid drill practice
of the present and passé composé on the indicated verbs.

- Vary the subjects, and have students transform the sentence.
  (Where needed, provide a predicate for the verb.)

  E.g., **Ils arrivent au stade. Nous.**   **Nous arrivons au stade.**
  Nous entrons. Vous.   **Vous entrez.**

- Have students transform the sentence to the negative.

  Je suis resté(e) au stade.   **Je ne suis pas resté(e) au stade.**

MEETING NATIONAL STANDARDS

GOAL 1:
COMMUNICATION

STANDARD 1.1
Interpersonal Communication:
Engaging in conversation

Have pairs of students imagine conversations between two people in the visual.

Avec un(e) camarade, composez un dialogue entre deux personnes sur le dessin.

MEETING NATIONAL STANDARDS

GOAL 1:
COMMUNICATION

STANDARD 1.3
Presentational Communication:
Presenting ideas

Have students pick one of the people in the visual, and imagine that the person is thinking aloud. What would he/she be saying?

Choisissez une des personnes du dessin, et imaginez qu'il/elle pense tout haut. Qu'est-ce qu'il/elle dit?

DESCRIPTION

Table settings illustrating the following items:

une serviette	**un couteau**
une assiette	**une fourchette**
un verre	**une cuillère**
une tasse	

Additional vocabulary:

une nappe	**une soucoupe**
un bouquet de fleurs	

Each setting is incomplete:

Sophie n'a pas de cuillère. Elle n'a pas de verre non plus.

François n'a pas d'assiette. Il n'a pas de tasse.

Olivier n'a pas de serviette.

Caroline n'a pas de couteau, pas de fourchette et pas de cuillère.

Source: NEW ART to illustrate vocabulary in Student Text, p. 144.

References and Activities in the Extended Teacher's Edition:
a) Lesson 9, p. T144

GOAL 4:

COMPARISONS

STANDARD 4.2

Comparing American and French culture

Have students observe how the silverware is placed in France:

- The spoon is placed above the plate (not next to the knife).
- The spoon and fork are placed concave-side down (which for Americans is "upside-down").

If you have access to actual French flatware, you can show how the designs and monograms on the spoons and forks are on the opposite side from in the United States.

Regardez bien comment on place les couverts (silverware) en France:
- *La cuillère est derrière l'assiette, et non pas à côté du couteau.*
- *La cuillère et la fourchette sont placées avec la partie concave vers le bas (downward) (On fait le contraire aux États-Unis).*

Si les cuillères et les fourchettes ont des dessins ou des monogrammes, sont-ils placés du même côté en France et aux États-Unis?

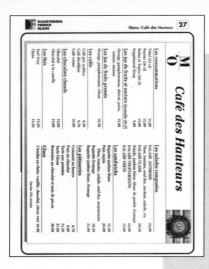

DESCRIPTION

Authentic menu to allow students to practice café dialogues, e.g.

— **S'il vous plaît, monsieur/mademoiselle!**
— **Vous désirez?**
— **Je voudrais une salade antiboise.**
— **Et comme boisson?**
— **Donnez-moi un Perrier, s'il vous plaît.**

Unfamiliar expressions:

supplément sirop	extra charge for flavored fruit syrup added to the water/soda
la cannelle	cinnamon
un oeuf dur	hard-boiled egg
le jambon blanc	cooked (as opposed to cured) ham
une noix	nut
un citron vert	lime
antibois	in the style of **Antibes** (on the French Riviera: **la Côte d'Azur**)
niçois	in the style of **Nice** (also on the Mediterranean)

Source: Menu from the "Café des Hauteurs" on the top floor of the Musée d'Orsay. Selections illustrate vocabulary in Student Text, p. 146.

References and Activities in the Extended Teacher's Edition:
a) Lesson 9, p. T146

GOAL 1:
COMMUNICATION

STANDARD 1.1
Interpersonal Communication:
Engaging in conversation

Have groups of two to four students imagine conversations at the Café des Hauteurs in which the guests decide what they want and place their order with the server.

Par groupes de deux ou quatre, imaginez une conversation au Café des Hauteurs: les clients décident ce qu'ils veulent, puis le commandent au garçon.

GOAL 3:
CONNECTIONS

STANDARD 3.2
Using French to find information:
Internet

Have students use the Internet to access Pariscope [http//:pariscope.fr] and find out additional information about the Musée d'Orsay: visiting days, hours, exhibits, other information.

Sur Internet, consultez Pariscope [http//:pariscope.fr] et cherchez des renseignements supplémentaires sur le Musée d'Orsay: jours et heures d'ouverture, etc.

Note: Website addresses may sometimes change; some addresses may not be accessible, depending on your computer setup

GOAL 4:
COMPARISONS

STANDARD 4.2
Comparing American and French culture

Have students read the menu carefully.

• Which items would they find at a local café-restaurant?

• Which items are not usually served in the United States?

Lisez attentivement le menu.

• *Quels éléments de ce menu peut-on trouver dans un café-restaurant de votre ville?*

• *Et quels éléments de ce menu ne sert-on généralement pas aux États-Unis?*

DESCRIPTION

Illustrations of breakfast foods:

de la confiture	**du beurre**
des céréales	**des oeufs sur le plat**
un oeuf [à la coque]	**du pain**
du chocolat chaud	**du lait**
du café	

Source: NEW ART to illustrate vocabulary in Student Text, p. 148.

References and Activities in the Extended Teacher's Edition:
a) Lesson 9, p. T148
b) Lesson 10, p. T160
c) Lesson 11, p. T169
d) Lesson 14, p. T206

REVIEW AND PRACTICE

Use Visual 28 to review and practice the use of the definite and partitive articles.

— **Est-ce que tu aimes le café?**
— **Oui, j'aime le café. (Non, je n'aime pas le café.)**

— **Est-ce que tu prends du café au petit déjeuner?**
— **Oui, je prends du café. (Non, je ne prends pas de café.)**

MEETING NATIONAL STANDARDS

GOAL 1:
COMMUNICATION

STANDARD 1.1
Interpersonal Communication: Engaging in conversation

Have students imagine that they have a French house guest. They make some breakfast suggestions and ask their guest what their preferences are. Have students play these roles with a classmate.

Vous avez un(e) invité(e) français(e) à la maison. Vous lui proposez certaines choses pour le petit déjeuner et vous lui demandez ce qu'il/elle préfère. Jouez ce dialogue avec un(e) camarade.

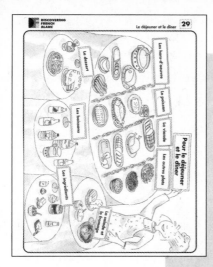

DESCRIPTION

Illustrations of foods served at lunch and dinner:

les hors-d'oeuvre:

la soupe	le jambon	le saucisson
le melon	le céleri	

le poisson:

le thon	la sole	le saumon

la viande:

le rosbif	le veau	le porc
le poulet		

les autres plats:

les frites	les spaghetti	le riz

la salade et le fromage:

le fromage	le yaourt	la salade

le dessert:

la glace	la tarte	le gâteau

les boissons:

le jus de raisin	l'eau minérale
le jus de pomme	l'eau
le lait	le jus d'orange

les ingrédients:

la moutarde	le poivre	le sucre
la mayonnaise	le ketchup	la margarine
le sel	le beurre	

Source: NEW ART to illustrate vocabulary in Student Text, p. 148.

References and Activities in the Extended Teacher's Edition:

a) Lesson 9, p. T148   c) Lesson 11, p. T169
b) Lesson 10, p. T160   d) Lesson 14, p. T206

REVIEW AND PRACTICE

Use Visual 28 to review and practice the use of the definite and partitive articles.

— **Est-ce que tu aimes la soupe?**
— **Oui, j'adore la soupe.**
  (Non, je n'aime pas la soupe)

— **Est-ce que tu voudrais de la soupe?**
— **Oui, je voudrais de la soupe, s'il te plaît. (Non, je ne voudrais pas de soupe, merci.)**

MEETING NATIONAL STANDARDS

GOAL 1:
COMMUNICATION

STANDARD 1.1
Interpersonal Communication:
Engaging in conversation

Have students imagine that they have a French house guest. They make some dinner suggestions and ask their guest what his/her preferences are. Have students play these roles with a classmate.

Vous avez un(e) invité(e) français(e) à la maison. Vous lui proposez certaines choses pour le dîner et vous lui demandez ce qu'il/elle préfère. Jouez ce dialogue avec un(e) camarade.

MEETING NATIONAL STANDARDS

GOAL 1:
CONNECTIONS

STANDARD 3.2
Using French to find information:
Internet

Have students use the Internet to access French recipes. They might want to try one out in conjunction with a cooking class.
[http//:www.cenaath.ce na.dgac.fr:80].

Sur Internet, consultez des recettes françaises. Et si vous suivez un cours de cuisine, préparez-en une!
[http//:www.cenaath.cena.dgac. fr:80]

Note: Website addresses may sometimes change; some addresses may not be accessible, depending on your computer setup.

GOAL 4:
COMPARISONS

STANDARD 4.1
Comparing English and French

Which of the food names are the same in both languages?

Which of these are English words which the French have borrowed?

Which of these are French words which the English have borrowed?

Quels aliments ont le même nom dans les deux langues?

Et dans cette catégorie, lesquels sont des mots anglais empruntés (borrowed) par le français?

Et lesquels sont des mots français empruntés par l'anglais?

30   Fruits et légumes

D E S C R I P T I O N

Le marché
Client and vendor at an open-air market.
Empty signs next to the fruits and vegetables can be used for identifying the items and/or for indicating prices.

fruits:
   pamplemousses
   oranges   pommes   poires
   fraises   cerises   bananes
légumes:
   salades   petits pois
   carottes   haricots
   tomates   pommes de terre

Source: Student text, p. 150
Note: Transparency does not have the names of the fruits and vegetables.

References and Activities in the Extended Teacher's Edition:
a) Lesson 9, p. T150
b) Lesson 11, p. T169
c) Lesson 18, p. T266

MEETING NATIONAL STANDARDS

GOAL 1:
COMMUNICATION

STANDARD 1.1
Interpersonal Communication:
Engaging in conversation

Imagine you are shopping in a French market. Your partner will play the role of the vendor. Carry out an appropriate conversation.

Vous faites les courses dans un marché en France. Un(e) camarade est le vendeur/la vendeuse. Imaginez un dialogue approprié.

31 Quel article?

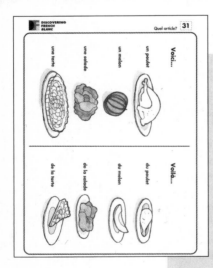

DESCRIPTION

Pairs of pictures contrasting the use of the indefinite and the partitive articles:

un poulet	**du poulet**
un melon	**du melon**
une salade	**de la salade**
une tarte	**de la tarte**

Source: Student text, p. 158

References and Activities in the Extended Teacher's Edition:
a) Lesson 10, p. T158

GOAL 4:
COMPARISONS

STANDARD 4.1
Comparing English and French

In English, these pictures would be described as "a melon," "some melon," etc.

One could consider the slice of melon as being "some of the melon," "a part of the melon."

In French, this notion of "some of the" is expressed simply by the words "of the": **du, de la.**

32 À la cantine

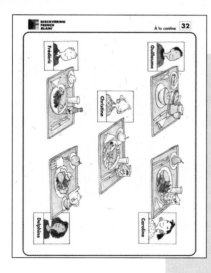

D E S C R I P T I O N

Illustrations of five students and their cafeteria trays.

Guillaume:	**de la soupe, un sandwich, du fromage, de l'eau**
Caroline:	**du rosbif (un steak), des haricots verts, une poire, du lait.**
Christine:	**du poisson, des frites, une pomme, du lait**
Frédéric:	**du poisson, des petits pois, une orange, du jus de tomate**
Delphine:	**du poulet, de la salade, une pomme, du thé**

Source: Student text, Activité 6, p. 170.

References and Activities in the Extended Teacher's Edition:
a) Lesson 11, p. T170

REVIEW AND PRACTICE

Vocabulary games:

- Have students answer questions according to the Visual:

    Qui mange du poisson et boit du lait? [Caroline]

- Have students indicate whether statements about the visual are true or false:

    Frédéric boit de l'eau. [faux]

MEETING NATIONAL STANDARDS

GOAL 1:

COMMUNICATION

STANDARD 1.3

Presentational Communication: Expressing preferences

Have students decide which of the five lunches they would prefer, and to explain why. If they do not like any of the lunches, have them describe their own choices.

Lequel de ces déjeuners préférez-vous? Pourquoi? Si vous n'en aimez aucun (none), dites ce que vous voulez manger.

DESCRIPTION

Illustrations of quantities/containers of food:

un litre de lait
une tranche de
jambon
une boîte de thon
une boîte de céréales
un kilo de pommes
une livre de beurre

une bouteille
d'eau minérale
un pot de mayonnaise
un paquet de café
un morceau de fromage
un sac d'oranges
une douzaine d'oeufs

Source: Vocabulary in Student text, p. 176.

References and Activities in the
Extended Teacher's Edition:
a) Lesson 12, p. T177

MEETING NATIONAL STANDARDS

GOAL 4:
COMPARISONS

STANDARD 4.2
Comparing American and French culture:
Measuring quantities

Which products in Visual 34 are sold in similar containers and/or quantities in both France and the United States?

Which are sold in different containers or quantities?

Quels produits sur ces dessins vend-on dans les mêmes récipients et sous les mêmes quantités en France et aux États-Unis?

Pour quels produits est-ce différent?

DESCRIPTION

Three students with trays showing various quantities of foods

Jean-Pierre: Il a **trop de** spaghetti.
Il a **peu de** cerises.

Guy: Il a **beaucoup de** spaghetti.
Il a **un peu de** salade.
Il a **beaucoup de** cerises.

Claire: Elle a **un peu de** spaghetti.
Elle a **beaucoup de** salade.
Elle a **assez de** cerises.

Source: NEW ART to illustrate vocabulary in Student Text, p. 178.

References and Activities in the Extended Teacher's Edition:
a) Lesson 23, p. T178

MEETING NATIONAL STANDARDS

GOAL 1:
COMMUNICATION

STANDARD 1.3
Presentational Communication:
Presenting ideas

Have students pick one of the people in the visual, and imagine that the person is thinking aloud. What would he/she be saying?

Choisissez une des personnes du dessin, et imaginez qu'il/elle pense tout haut. Qu'est-ce qu'il/elle dit?

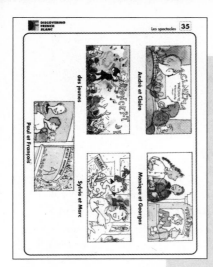

DESCRIPTION

Five scenes showing young people at different types of shows and events.

André et Claire vont au cinéma **pour voir un film.**

Monique et Georges vont au théâtre **pour voir une pièce de théâtre** et **pour voir leurs actrices et leurs acteurs favoris.**

Des jeunes vont au concert **pour entendre un orchestre/une chanteuse.**

Sylvie et Marc vont au musée **pour voir une exposition.**

Paul et François vont au stade **pour assister à un match,** et **pour voir les joueurs de leur équipe favorite.**

Source: Illustrated vocabulary from Student Text, p. 194.

References and Activities in the Extended Teacher's Edition:
a) Lesson 13, p. T194
b) Lesson 22, p. T309

MEETING NATIONAL STANDARDS

GOAL 1:
COMMUNICATION

STANDARD 1.1
Interpersonal Communication:
Engaging in conversation

Have pairs of students imagine conversations between two people in the visual.

Avec un(e) camarade, composez un dialogue entre deux personnes sur le dessin.

MEETING NATIONAL STANDARDS

GOAL 3:
CONNECTIONS

STANDARD 3.2
Using French to find information: Internet

Have students consult Pariscope on the internet [http//pariscope.fr/] and find out information about current Paris events: museum shows, concerts, etc. Have them select the one they would like to see or attend.

Sur Internet, consultez Pariscope [http//pariscope.fr/] et renseignez-vous sur des activités culturelles courantes à Paris: expositions dans les musées, concerts, etc. Choisissez une exposition que vous aimeriez voir, un concert auquel vous voudriez assister, etc.

Note: Website addresses may sometimes change; some addresses may not be accessible, depending on your computer setup.

36 Qu'est-ce qu'on fait?

DESCRIPTION

Collage of announcements for recent events in Paris.

Unfamiliar expressions:

LOC PAR TEL	= **location par téléphone:** reservations by telephone
un parfum	flavor
un championnat	championship playoff

Source: NEW ART: ads adapted from Paris magazines, to accompany and illustrate dialogues in Student Text, pp. 198-199.

References and Activities in the Extended Teacher's Edition:
a) Lesson 13, p. T198

MEETING NATIONAL STANDARDS

GOAL 1:
COMMUNICATION

STANDARD 1.1
Interpersonal Communication:
Engaging in conversation

Have pairs of students discuss where they want to go this weekend, using the suggestions on Visual 36.

Avec un(e) camarade, discutez ce que vous voulez faire ce weekend. Basez-vous sur les images montrées.

MEETING NATIONAL STANDARDS

GOAL 1:
COMMUNICATION

STANDARD 1.1
Interpersonal Communication:
Communicating via e-mail

Have two students (either in the same class, or in different classes) communicate back and forth via e-mail to decide what they would like to do on Saturday. Have them print out their conversation.

Avec un(e) camarade, de votre classe ou d'une autre classe, correspondez par courrier électronique pour décider ce que vous allez faire samedi. Imprimez votre conversation.

MEETING NATIONAL STANDARDS

GOAL 3:
CONNECTIONS

STANDARD 3.2
Using French to find information:
Internet

Have students use the Internet to access Pariscope [http//:pariscope.fr] and find out other types of activities they might do or places they might go this weekend.

Sur Internet, consultez Pariscope [http//pariscope.fr/] et regardez quels autres genres d'activités ou d'endroits sont aussi des possibilités pour ce weekend.

Note: Website addresses may sometimes change; some addresses may not be accessible, depending on your computer setup.

DESCRIPTION

Illustrations show people rendering each other services:

prêter: **Sylvie prête son compact à Paul.**

montrer: **Bernard montre ses photos à ses cousins.**

présenter: **Michel présente Hélène à sa mère.**

rendre: **Marie rend le livre à Jean. Elle lui rend son livre.**

donner: **Éric donne son adresse à Pauline.**

apporter: **Michel apporte un énorme cadeau à sa mère.**

Source: NEW ART to illustrate vocabulary in Student Text, p. 205.

References and Activities in the
Extended Teacher's Edition:
a) Lesson 14, p. T205
b) Lesson 16, p. T226
c) Lesson 35, p. T472

MEETING NATIONAL STANDARDS

GOAL 1:
COMMUNICATION

STANDARD 1.1
Interpersonal Communication: Engaging in conversation

Have pairs of students imagine conversations between two people in the visual.

Avec un(e) camarade, composez un dialogue entre deux personnes sur le dessin.

GOAL 1:
COMMUNICATION

STANDARD 1.3
Presentational Communication:
Presenting ideas

Have students pick one of the people in the visual, and imagine that the person is thinking aloud. What would he/she be saying?

Choisissez une des personnes du dessin, et imaginez qu'il/elle pense tout haut. Qu'est-ce qu'il/elle dit?

38 Les gens et les choses

DESCRIPTION

Illustrations show people engaged in the following activities:

Dans la chambre de Claire — Claire, Marie, et Sandrine

chercher: **Claire cherche sa montre sous le bureau.**

trouver: **Marie trouve la montre de Claire [sur l'étagère].**

garder: **Sandrine veut garder le magazine qu'elle a dans les mains.**

Au parc des sports — Daniel et Christophe

laisser: **Christophe a laissé sa raquette à la maison.**

oublier: **Il a oublié ses lunettes de soleil dans le bus.**

Source: NEW ART to illustrate vocabulary in Student Text, p. 220.

References and Activities in the Extended Teacher's Edition:
a) Lesson 15, p. T220

MEETING NATIONAL STANDARDS

GOAL 1:
COMMUNICATION

STANDARD 1.1
Interpersonal Communication:
Engaging in conversation

Have pairs of students imagine conversations between two people in the visual.

Avec un(e) camarade, composez un dialogue entre deux personnes sur le dessin.

MEETING NATIONAL STANDARDS

GOAL 1:
COMMUNICATION

STANDARD 1.3
Presentational Communication:
Presenting ideas

Have students pick one of the people in the visual, and imagine that the person is thinking aloud. What would he/she be saying?

Choisissez une des personnes du dessin, et imaginez qu'il/elle pense tout haut. Qu'est-ce qu'il/elle dit?

DESCRIPTION

Three scenes to illustrate people reading, writing, and talking.

On lit …
   des bandes dessinées
   un roman
   une histoire
   une revue, un magazine
   le journal

On écrit …
   une lettre
   une carte (postale)
   un journal

**On dit … que le film est génial, que les acteurs
sont fantastiques.**
   Est-ce que ces gens disent la vérité?

Source: NEW ART to illustrate vocabulary in Student
Text, p. 225.

*References and Activities in the
Extended Teacher's Edition:*
a) Lesson 16, p. T225

MEETING NATIONAL STANDARDS

GOAL 1:
   COMMUNICATION

STANDARD 1.1
   Interpersonal Communication:
   Engaging in conversation

Have pairs of students imagine
conversations between two people
in the visual.

*Avec un(e) camarade, composez un
dialogue entre deux personnes sur le
dessin.*

MEETING NATIONAL STANDARDS

GOAL 1:
COMMUNICATION

STANDARD 1.1
Interpersonal Communication:
Engaging in discussion

Have groups of students imagine they are the young people in the third scene of the visual. They discuss a recent movie they have seen, reporting what others are saying about it.

Les jeunes de la troisième scène parlent d'un film récent qu'ils ont vu. Ils mentionnent aussi ce que d'autres personnes en disent. Avec des camarades, jouez leur conversation.

MEETING NATIONAL STANDARDS

GOAL 1:
COMMUNICATION

STANDARD 1.3
Presentational Communication:
Presenting ideas

Have students pick one of the people in the first scene, and imagine that the person is talking about something he/she has just read.

Choisissez une des personnes de la première scène. Imaginez qu'il/elle parle de quelque chose qu'il/elle vient de lire. Qu'est-ce qu'il/elle dit?

MEETING NATIONAL STANDARDS

GOAL 1:
COMMUNICATION

STANDARD 1.3
Presentational Communication:
Personal correspondence

Have students pick one of the people in the second scene, and continue writing the card or letter.

Choisissez une des personnes de la deuxième scène, et continuez la carte ou la lettre.

DESCRIPTION

Composite drawing illustrating individual sports.

sports d'hiver:
le ski   le patinage

sports d'été:
la voile   le VTT
le surf   la planche à roulettes
le ski nautique   le patin à roulettes
  [le bateau]   le jogging
la planche à voile   l'aérobic
la natation   la gymnastique
la marche à pied   l'équitation
le vélo

Es-tu sportif/sportive?
Est-ce que tu fais du sport?
Quels sports est-ce que tu pratiques?
Pierre court.
Michèle et ses copines font de l'aérobic.

Source: NEW ART to illustrate vocabulary in Student Text, p. 256.

References and Activities in the Extended Teacher's Edition:
a) Lesson 17, p. T256
b) Lesson 18, p. T266
c) Lesson 20, p. T2887

MEETING NATIONAL STANDARDS

GOAL 1:
COMMUNICATION

STANDARD 1.1
Interpersonal Communication:
Engaging in conversation

Have pairs of students imagine conversations between two people in the visual.

Avec un(e) camarade, composez un dialogue entre deux personnes sur le dessin.

MEETING NATIONAL STANDARDS

GOAL 1:
COMMUNICATION

STANDARD 1.3
Presentational Communication:
Narrating in the past

Have students use Visual 40 as a point of departure to talk or write about some of the things they did on a recent vacation (real or imagined).

En utilisant le vocabulaire de ce dessin, racontez ce que vous avez fait pendant vos dernières vacances (réelles ou imaginaires). Faites-le par écrit ou oralement.

41 Les parties du corps

DESCRIPTION

Illustrations showing parts of the body and selected movements.

le corps:

un doigt	le coeur	le genou
la main	le dos	le pied
le bras	le ventre/l'estomac	
l'épaule	la jambe	

la tête et la figure:

les cheveux	le nez	une dent
un oeil	une oreille	le cou
(les yeux)	la bouche	

un peu de gymnastique:
Je lève le bras droit.
Je lève le bras gauche.
Je plie les jambes.
Je mets les mains derrière le dos.
Je mets les mains sur la tête.

Source: Art and vocabulary from Student Text, p. 258

References and Activities in the Extended Teacher's Edition:
a) Lesson 17, p. T258

GOAL 4:

COMPARISONS

STANDARD 4.1

Comparing English and French:
Vocabulary expansion
increase one's English vocabulary

Have students in groups see how many English words or expressions they can find which are related to the vocabulary of Visual 41,. e.g.,

genou	genuflect
pied	pedal

Combien de mots ou d'expressions en anglais pouvez-vous trouver qui ressemblent aux mots de ce vocabulaire?

DESCRIPTION

Nine drawings to illustrate health vocabulary.

— **Ça va?**

— **Non, ça ne va pas. Je ne suis pas en forme.**

Je suis en mauvaise santé. Je ne me sens pas bien.

— **Qu'est-ce que tu as?**

[dame]	**Je suis fatiguée.**
[monsieur]	**J'ai un rhume.**
[homme au lit]	**J'ai la grippe. Je suis malade.**
[jeune fille]	**J'ai mal à la tête.**
[jeune homme]	**J'ai mal au ventre.**
[jeune fille]	**J'ai mal au dos.**
[garçon]	**J'ai mal à l'oreille.**

— **Ça va?**

— **Oui, ça va. Ça va mieux.**

[jeune fille qui court]

Je suis en bonne santé.

Je me sens bien.

[garçon qui joue au basket]

Je suis en forme.

Source: NEW ART to illustrate vocabulary in Student Text, p. 260.

References and Activities in the Extended Teacher's Edition:
a) Lesson 17, p. T260

GOAL 1:
COMMUNICATION

STANDARD 1.1
Interpersonal Communication:
Engaging in conversation

Have pairs of students imagine conversations between two people in the visual in which each one complains of a health problem.

Avec un(e) camarade, choisissez deux personnes du dessin. Chaque personne parle de son problème de santé. Jouez ce dialogue.

43 Les occupations de la journée

DESCRIPTION

Daily activities suggesting reflexive verbs.

6h45	Patrick se réveille.
7h00	Il se lève.
7h15	Il se lave.
7h30	Il s'habille.
4h30	Il se promène avec un copain.
5h30	Il se repose.
9h00	Il se lave les cheveux.
10h00	Il se couche.

Source: NEW ART to illustrate vocabulary in Student Text, p. 276.

References and Activities in the Extended Teacher's Edition:
a) Lesson 19, p. T276
b) Lesson 20, p. T286
c) Lesson 36, p. T482

MEETING NATIONAL STANDARDS

GOAL 1:
COMMUNICATION

STANDARD 1.1
Interpersonal Communication:
Engaging in conversation

Have pairs of students imagine conversations between two people in the visual.

Avec un(e) camarade, composez un dialogue entre deux personnes sur le dessin.

MEETING NATIONAL STANDARDS

GOAL 1:
COMMUNICATION

STANDARD 1.3
Presentational Communication:
Writing stories

Have students use Visual 43 as a point of departure for writing a short description of a day in the life of a friend (real or imaginary).

- In the present tense, this would be a description of their friend's daily routine.
- In the imperfect, it would be a description of their friends's routine at some point in the past.
- In the passé composé, it would be a description of what happened on one particular day.

En vous basant sur ce dessin, racontez par écrit la journée d'un(e) de vos ami(e)s (réel(le) ou imaginaire):

- *Au présent, description de sa routine quotidienne (daily) maintenant.*
- *À l'imparfait, la routine quotidienne, mais dans le passé.*

- *Au passé composé, une description de ce qui s'est passé (happened) un jour.*

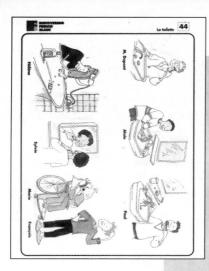

DESCRIPTION

Six pictures illustrating personal care.

M. Dupont:	**Il se rase.** **Il a un rasoir.**
Alain:	**Il se lave les mains.** **Il utilise du savon.**
Paul:	**Il se lave les dents. Il se brosse les dents.** **Il a une brosse à dents et du dentifrice.**
Hélène:	**Elle se lave les cheveux.** **Elle a du shampooing.**
Sylvie:	**Sylvie se maquille.** **Elle met du rouge à lèvres.**
Marie:	**Elle se brosse les cheveux.** **Elle a une brosse à cheveux.**
François:	**Il se peigne.** **Il a un peigne.**

Source: NEW ART to illustrate vocabulary in Student Text, p. 276.

References and Activities in the Extended Teacher's Edition:
a) Lesson 19, p. T278

REVIEW AND PRACTICE

Use Visual 44 to practice present and passé composé forms of reflexive verbs.

[pointing to Hélène]

Elle se lave les cheveux. Nous
Nous nous lavons les cheveux. Moi
Je me lave les cheveux. etc.

[pointing to Marie]

Elle s'est brossé les cheveux. Nous
Nous nous sommes brossé les cheveux. Moi
Je me suis brossé les cheveux. etc.

MEETING NATIONAL STANDARDS

GOAL 1:
COMMUNICATION

STANDARD 1.3
Presentational Communication:
Describing one's plans

Have students pick one of the people in the visual, and have that person describe his/her plans for the day.

Vous êtes une de ces personnes. Décrivez vos projets pour la journée.

DESCRIPTION

Street scene illustrating certain reflexive verbs:

s'arrêter	**Madame Lucet s'arrête brusquement. [Son chien s'arrête aussi.]**
s'excuser	**Monsieur Dupont s'excuse. [Il a renversé un pot de tulipes.]**
se dépêcher	**Monsieur Dupont se dépêche. [Il est en retard pour un rendez-vous.]**
s'amuser	**Les jeunes au café s'amusent. [Ils trouvent la scène très drôle.]**
se souvenir (de)	**Roger est dans une cabine téléphonique. Il ne se souvient pas du numéro de Claire. [Il l'a oublié.]**

Source: NEW ART to illustrate vocabulary in Student Text, p. 284.

References and Activities in the Extended Teacher's Edition:
a) Lesson 20, p. T284

MEETING NATIONAL STANDARDS

GOAL 1:
COMMUNICATION

STANDARD 1.1
Interpersonal Communication:
Engaging in conversation

Have pairs of students imagine conversations between two people in the visual.

Avec un(e) camarade, composez un dialogue entre deux personnes sur le dessin.

MEETING NATIONAL STANDARDS

GOAL 1:
COMMUNICATION

STANDARD 1.3
Presentational Communication:
Narrating past events

Have students imagine that they were witnesses of the scene in Visual 45. Have them describe what happened, either by telling the story to a group of friends, or by writing about it in a letter.

Vous êtes témoin (witness) de cette scène. Décrivez ce qui s'est passé (happened). Vous pouvez raconter la scène à un groupe de vos camarades, ou la décrire dans une lettre.

MEETING NATIONAL STANDARDS

GOAL 4:
COMPARISONS

STANDARD 4.2
Comparing American and French culture

Does the scene in Visual 45 take place in the United States or in France? How can you tell?

Est-ce que cette scène a lieu (takes place) aux États-Unis ou en France? Comment le savez-vous?

DESCRIPTION

Scene of a woman looking at pictures displayed in a real estate office.

- **une maison individuelle dans un village**
- **un appartement dans un quartier ancien du centre-ville**
- **une ferme à la campagne**
- **un immeuble moderne dans un quartier moderne dans la banlieue**

Source: NEW ART to illustrate vocabulary in Student Text, p. 300.

References and Activities in the Extended Teacher's Edition:
a) Lesson 21, p. T300

MEETING NATIONAL STANDARDS

GOAL 1:
COMMUNICATION

STANDARD 1.1
Interpersonal Communication: Engaging in conversation

Have pairs of students imagine conversations between two people in the visual.

Avec un(e) camarade, composez un dialogue entre deux personnes sur le dessin.

MEETING NATIONAL STANDARDS

GOAL 1:
COMMUNICATION

STANDARD 1.3
Presentational Communication:
Expressing one's preferences

Have students imagine that they are looking for a place to live in France for a year. Which of the places shown in the realtor's window would they be most interested in and why? Have them explain their choice, either orally or in writing.

Imaginez que vous cherchez un endroit en France où habiter pendant un an. Lequel des endroits montrés ici préférez-vous? Pourquoi? (Exercice écrit ou oral)

47 Les parties de la maison

DESCRIPTION

Illustrations of house vocabulary:
Les parties de la maison:

le garage	le rez-de-chaussée
le jardin	le premier étage
le sous-sol	le grenier
[la cave]	le toit
les escaliers	
(un escalier)	

Une pièce:

le mur	la porte
la fenêtre	le couloir
le plafond	une clé
le sol	

Source: Art and vocabulary from Student Text, p. 301.

References and Activities in the Extended Teacher's Edition:
a) Lesson 21, p. T301

GOAL 4:
COMPARISONS

STANDARD 4.1
Comparing English and French:
Vocabulary expansion

Have students in groups see how many English words or expressions they can find which are related to the vocabulary of Visual 47, e.g.,

mur	mural
porte	portal

Combien de mots ou d'expressions en anglais pouvez-vous trouver qui ressemblent aux mots de ce vocabulaire?

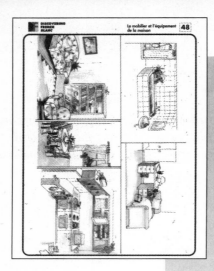

DESCRIPTION

The rooms of the house and their furnishings:

les pièces de la maison:
　la salle de bains
　　une douche　　　　　un lavabo
　　une baignoire　　　[des toilettes/les WC]
　　une glace

　une chambre à coucher
　　un placard　　　　　une lampe
　　un meuble　　　　　un lit
　　un bureau

　le salon/le living
　　un tableau　　　　　un fauteuil
　　un sofa　　　　　　un tapis
　　une étagère

　la salle à manger
　　une table　　　　　des rideaux
　　une chaise

　la cuisine
　　un grille-pain　　　un réfrigérateur
　　des placards　　　　une machine à laver
　　un évier　　　　　　un four à micro-ondes
　　une cuisinière　　　un appareil
　　un four

Source: Art and vocabulary from Student Text, p. 301 and pp 302-303.

*References and Activities in the
Extended Teacher's Edition:*
a) Lesson 21, p. 302, p. 303

MEETING NATIONAL STANDARDS

GOAL 1:
COMMUNICATION

STANDARD 1.3
Presentational Communication:
Expressing preferences

Have students decide which room of the house in Visual 48 they like best, and to explain their choice.

Quelle pièce de cette maison préférez-vous? Pourquoi?

MEETING NATIONAL STANDARDS

GOAL 4:
COMPARISONS

STANDARD 1.1
Comparing English and French

- Which words illustrated in Visual 48 have been borrowed from English by the French? e.g., le living, les WC [water closets]
- Have students in groups see how many English words or expressions they can find which are related to the vocabulary of Visual 48, e.g.,

four	furnace
onde *(wave)*	undulate

Quels mots illustrés ici le français a-t-il empruntés à l'anglais?

Combien de mots ou d'expressions en anglais pouvez-vous trouver qui ressemblent aux mots de ce vocabulaire?

DESCRIPTION

Seven drawings showing habitual actions in the past:

En 1995, Alain et Lucie habitaient à la Martinique.

Alain avait neuf ans. Il jouait souvent avec son petit chien.

Lucie avait onze ans. Elle avait un petit chat qui s'appelait Mimi.

Tous les matins, Alain et Lucie allaient à l'école.

Alain allait à pied.

Lucie prenait le bus.

Le weekend, Alain jouait au foot avec ses copains.

Ils s'amusaient bien.

Lucie allait à la plage avec des amis.

Ils jouaient au volley.

Ils nageaient.

Souvent Lucie et sa copine se promenaient à vélo.

Alain se couchait à huit heures et demie. Il voulait être astronaute.

Lucie se couchait plus tard. Elle voulait être actrice de cinéma.

Source: NEW ART to illustrate use of the imperfect, Student Text, p. 319.

References and Activities in the Extended Teacher's Edition:
a) Lesson 23, p. T319
b) Lesson 32, p. T432

As a warm-up, have students describe the activities in Visual 49 in the present tense.

Décrivez ces activités au présent.

MEETING NATIONAL STANDARDS

GOAL 1:
COMMUNICATION

STANDARD 1.1
Interpersonal Communication:
Engaging in conversation

Have pairs of students imagine conversations between two people in the visual.

Avec un(e) camarade, composez un dialogue entre deux personnes sur le dessin.

MEETING NATIONAL STANDARDS

GOAL 1:
COMMUNICATION

STANDARD 1.3
Presentational Communication:
Narrating past activities

Have students use Visual 49 as a point of departure to describe what they used to do when they were ten years old.

En vous basant sur ces scènes, dites ce que vous faisiez quand vous aviez dix ans.

DESCRIPTION

Paired illustrations showing Monsieur Michel before and after he won ten million francs at the lottery.

Maintenant ...	Avant ...
M. Michel vit à la campagne.	Il vivait en ville.
Il habite un joli château.	Il habitait une petite maison.
Il a une belle voiture de sport.	Il avait un vieux vélo
Il a beaucoup d'amis.	Il vivait seul.
Il dîne dans les grands restaurants.	Il dînait dans le bist de son quartier.
Il va à la pêche avec son nouveau bateau.	Il allait à la pêche près de sa maison
Pour partir en vacances, il prend l'avion.	Pour partir en vacances, il parta à vélo.
Il passe ses vacances sur la Côte d'Azur.	Il passait ses vacances à la campagne.
Il descend dans un grand hôtel de luxe.	Il faisait du camping sauvage.

Source: NEW ART to illustrate use of the imperfect, cf. Activité 7, Student Text, p. 320.

References and Activities in the Extended Teacher's Edition:
a) Lesson 23, p. T320

MEETING NATIONAL STANDARDS

GOAL 1: COMMUNICATION

STANDARD 1.1
Interpersonal Communication: Engaging in conversation

Have pairs of students imagine the conversation between M. Michel and his guest in the upper left-hand picture.

Regardez le dessin en haut à gauche. Avec un(e) camarade, imaginez le dialogue entre M. Michel et son invité.

MEETING NATIONAL STANDARDS

GOAL 1: COMMUNICATION

STANDARD 1.3
Presentational Communication: Presenting ideas

Have students pick one of the pictures, and imagine what M. Michel is thinking.

Choisissez un des dessins et imaginez ce que pense M. Michel.

MEETING NATIONAL STANDARDS

GOAL 4: COMPARISONS

STANDARD 4.2
Comparing American and French culture

These scenes depict stereotypes of how the French view the simple life of the working man, and the life of a high-spender who has just won a fortune at the lottery. If similar scenes were drawn by an American artist for American readers, how would they be modified?

Ces scènes montrent de façon stéréotypée comment les Français imaginent la vie simple des travailleurs, et la vie des gens qui viennent de gagner une fortune à la loterie. Si un artiste américain dessinait ce genre de scènes pour un public américain, qu'est-ce qui serait (would be) différent?

DESCRIPTION

Composite drawing showing what members of the Dumas family were doing at 5:30 when Philippe phoned their house.

À cinq heures et demie, Philippe a téléphoné chez les Dumas.
Personne n'a répondu.

- **Monsieur Dumas jouait au foot avec son fils Henri.**
- **Lise et François jouaient au volley avec leurs copains.**
- **Isabelle réparait son vélo.**
- **Madame Dumas travaillait dans le jardin. [Elle faisait du jardinage.]**
- **Jean-Claude lavait sa voiture.**

Source: NEW ART to illustrate use of the imperfect for on-going activities, Student Text, p. 322.

References and Activities in the
Extended Teacher's Edition:
a) Lesson 23, p. T322

REVIEW AND PRACTICE

As a warm-up, have students describe the activities in Visual 51 in the present tense.

Décrivez ces activités au présent.

GOAL 1:
COMMUNICATION

STANDARD 1.1
Interpersonal Communication:
Engaging in conversation

Have pairs of students imagine conversations between Philippe and one of the people in the visual. Philippe is wondering why nobody answered the phone.

Note: Be sure that Philippe's conversations with M. and Mme Dumas use the **vous** *form.*

Avec un(e) camarade, imaginez un dialogue entre Philippe et une des personnes du dessin. Philippe se demande (wonders) *pourquoi personne n'a répondu au téléphone.*

MEETING NATIONAL STANDARDS

GOAL 1:
COMMUNICATION

STANDARD 1.3
Presentational Communication:
Presenting ideas: role-play

Have students pick one of the people in the visual, and imagine that the person is thinking aloud. What would he/she be saying?

Choisissez une des personnes du dessin, et imaginez qu'il/elle pense tout haut. Qu'est-ce qu'il/elle dit?

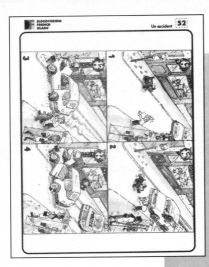

DESCRIPTION

Sequence of four pictures illustrating an automobile accident.

- **Scène 1:**
  Il était deux heures moins cinq.
  Il neigeait.
  Il y avait deux personnes dans la rue.
  Le garçon appelait son chien.
  Une voiture approchait.

- **Scène 2:**
  Il y avait une personne dans la voiture.
  Le conducteur était un jeune homme.
  Le chien a traversé la rue.

- **Scène 3:**
  Un accident a eu lieu.
  [La voiture a freiné.]
  La voiture a heurté le panneau de stop.
  Elle n'est pas entrée dans le magasin
    d'antiquités.
  La dame était témoin de l'accident.
  Elle a téléphoné à la police.

- **Scène 4:**
  Le conducteur est sorti de la voiture.
  Le garçon est parti avec son chien.
  Une voiture de police est arrivée.

Source: Art and descriptions from Activité 1, Student Text, pp. 328-329.

*References and Activities in the
Extended Teacher's Edition:*
a) Lesson 24, p. T328
b) Lesson 24, p. T330

As a warm-up plus vocabulary review, have students describe the four scenes in the present tense. Draw their attention to the details in the drawings.

Décrivez ces quatre scènes au présent. N'oubliez pas de donner des détails!

MEETING NATIONAL STANDARDS

GOAL 4:
COMPARISONS

STANDARD 4.1
Comparing English and French

a) How does English express on-going actions in the past? [e.g., The boy was calling his dog. Past progressive.] Does this verb consist of one word or two?
What is the corresponding verb tense in French? [The imperfect: Le garçon appelait son chien.] Does this verb consist of one word or two?

b) How does English express a specific past action? [e.g., The dog crossed the street. Simple past.] Does this verb consist of one word or two? What about in the negative?
What is the corresponding verb tense in French? [The passé composé: Le chien a traversé la rue.] Does this verb consist of one word or two?

a) *Comment exprime-t-on en anglais des actions progressives dans le passé? Est-ce que ce verbe consiste en un mot ou deux? Quel est le temps (tense) correspondant en français?*

b) *Comment exprime-t-on en anglais une action spécifique au passé? Est-ce que ce verbe consiste en un mot ou deux? Et pour la négation?*

Quel est le temps correspondant en français? Est-ce que ce verbe consiste en un mot ou deux?

DESCRIPTION

Clothing display at a department store.

Au rayon des vêtements

- **Pour hommes et femmes**

un manteau	une chemise
une veste	un pull
un pantalon	un jean
un blazer	un blouson
un imper	des chaussettes
(un imperméable)	

- **Pour femmes**

un tailleur	une robe
un chemisier	des collants
une jupe	

- **Pour hommes**

un costume	une cravate

Source: Illustrated vocabulary from the Student Text, p. 346.

References and Activities in the Extended Teacher's Edition:
a) Lesson 25, p. 346

REVIEW AND PRACTICE

- Use Visual 53 to review colors.
  - **De quelle couleur est l'imperméable?**
  - **Il est jaune.**

- Use Visual 53 with Lesson 34 to review the conditional and practice **pour + infinitive**.
  - **Quand est-ce que tu porterais ce vêtement?** *(pointing to an item on the visual)*
  - **Je porterais ce blouson pour faire une promenade à la campagne.**

GOAL 4:
COMMUNICATION

STANDARD 4.1
Comparing English and French

- Which of the names of items of clothing are borrowed from the English?
  [**un jean, un blazer, un pull(over)**]
- Which names are false cognates?
  [**une robe** is a *dress,* not a *robe;*
  un costume is a *suit,* not a *costume;*
  une veste is a *jacket,* not a *vest*]

Quels noms de vêtements sont empruntés (borrowed) à l'anglais?

Quels noms sont des faux-amis?

54 Les vêtements de sport et les chaussures

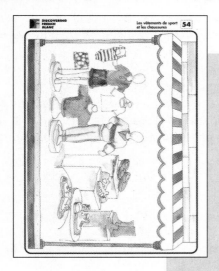

DESCRIPTION

- **Au rayon des vêtements de sports**
un polo	un short
un maillot de bain	un sweat
un tee-shirt	un survêtement

- **Au rayon des chaussures**
des chaussures	des baskets
des sandales	des tennis
des bottes	

Source: Illustrated vocabulary from the Student Text, p. 347.

References and Activities in the Extended Teacher's Edition:
a) Lesson 25, p. 347

REVIEW AND PRACTICE

Use the items in Visual 53 to review French sports.

— **Quand est-ce que tu mets un maillot de bain?**
— **Je mets un maillot de bain quand je nage, quand je fais de la planche à voile, etc.**

MEETING NATIONAL STANDARDS

GOAL 4:
COMPARISONS

STANDARD 4.1
Comparing English and French

- Which of the items of clothing have names borrowed from English?
- Do the corresponding sports also have English names in French? [**le golf, le tennis, le basket(ball), le polo, le foot(ball)**]
- Note that sports which did not come from England have French names, and that the items of clothing also have French names: e.g.,

  la natation: un maillot de bain

Quels noms de vêtements sont empruntés à l'anglais?

Est-ce que les sports correspondants ont aussi un nom anglais en français?

Remarquez que les sports qui ne sont pas originaires d'Angleterre ont un nom français, et que les vêtements correspondants ont aussi un nom français.

55 (o) Les accessoires et les articles personnels *(overlay with blank price tags)*

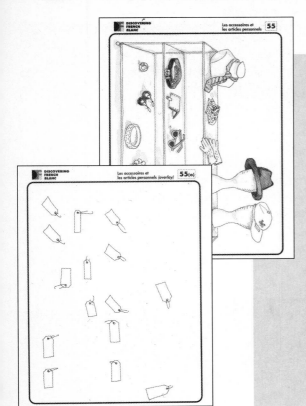

D E S C R I P T I O N

A display of accessories.

- **les accessoires**

une cravate	une ceinture
un foulard	un portefeuille
des gants	des lunettes de soleil
un chapeau	un sac
une casquette	un parapluie

- **les bijoux**

une bague	un collier
des boucles	une chaîne avec une
d'oreille	médaille
un bracelet	

Source: Illustrated vocabulary from the Student Text, p. 348.

References and Activities in the Extended Teacher's Edition:
a) Lesson 25, p. T348
b) Lesson 26, p. T356

REVIEW AND PRACTICE

Use the overlay to review numbers. Have students suggest prices and then dictate these to a classmate who will write them on the transparency.

Révisez les nombres: suggérez des prix pour les articles montrés.

MEETING NATIONAL STANDARDS

GOAL 1:
COMMUNICATION

STANDARD 1.1
Interpersonal Communication:
Engaging in conversation

Have pairs of students imagine conversations between two people trying to decide on a birthday present for a friend.

Avec un(e) camarade, imaginez un dialogue entre deux personnes qui veulent acheter un cadeau d'anniversaire pour un copain/une copine.

 MEETING NATIONAL STANDARDS

GOAL 1:
COMMUNICATION

STANDARD 1.3
Presentational Communication:
Expressing preferences

Have students pick one of the items in the visual, and explain why they would purchase that particular item and on what occasions they would wear/use it.

Choisissez un des objets montrés et expliquez pourquoi vous l'achèteriez et quand vous aller le porter ou l'utiliser.

DESCRIPTION

Group of people waiting for the bus. They are all wearing different clothes.

Ces gens attendent le bus. Le petit chien de Mme Mercier veut courir après le pigeon.

- **Sylvie porte un chemisier violet, une jupe à pois et des tennis.**
- **Jean porte un pull bleu, une veste à carreaux, un pantalon à rayures et des chaussures marron.**
- **Corinne porte une robe à fleurs. [Elle a un ruban dans les cheveux.]**
- **Philippe porte une chemise à rayures, un jean avec une ceinture blanche et des sandales.**
- **Mme Mercier porte un tailleur rouge, un joli chapeau, un sac noir, [des bas et des chaussures à talon].**
  (Elle tire sur la laisse de son chien.)
- **M. Lucet porte un costume à rayures et un parapluie.**
- **Mlle Rochette porte une robe jaune et un collier sous son imperméable.**
- **Olivier porte un blouson vert sur son survêtement bleu. Il porte aussi des baskets.**

Source: NEW ART to illustrate vocabulary in Student Text, p. 349.

References and Activities in the Extended Teacher's Edition:
a) Lesson 25, p. T349

REVIEW AND PRACTICE

Guessing game: One student describes what a person in the visual is wearing, and the class guesses the corresponding person's name.

Un(e) camarade va décrire ce que porte une des personnes du dessin. Devinez qui est cette personne.

MEETING NATIONAL STANDARDS

GOAL 1:
COMMUNICATION

STANDARD 1.1
Interpersonal Communication:
Engaging in conversation

Have pairs of students imagine conversations between two people in the visual.

Avec un(e) camarade, composez un dialogue entre deux personnes sur le dessin.

MEETING NATIONAL STANDARDS

GOAL 1:
COMMUNICATION

STANDARD 1.3
Presentational Communication:
Presenting ideas

Have students pick one of the people in the visual, and imagine that the person is thinking aloud. What would he/she be saying?

Choisissez une des personnes du dessin, et imaginez qu'il/elle pense tout haut. Qu'est-ce qu'il/elle dit?

MEETING NATIONAL STANDARDS

GOAL 1:
COMMUNICATION

STANDARD 1.3
Presentational Communication:
Narration in the past

What happened next? Did the dog stop, or did he knock someone over? Narrate the scene in the past tense.

Qu'est-ce qui s'est passé (happened) après? Est-ce que le chien s'est arrêté, ou est-ce qu'il a renversé (knock over) quelqu'un? Racontez la scène au passé.

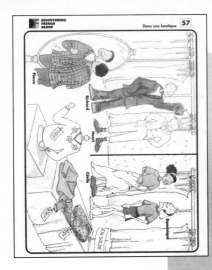

DESCRIPTION

Young people are trying out clothes at a department store.

The illustrations may be used as the basis of conversations using the following expressions:

— **Vous désirez?**
— **Je cherche [un pantalon].**
   Je voudrais essayer [cette jupe].
— **Quelle est votre taille?**
— **Je fais [du 40].**

— **Est-ce que [ce costume] vous va?**
— **Oui, il me va bien.**
   Non, il ne me va pas.
   Non, il est trop | **grand ≠ petit**
   | **court ≠ long**
   | **étroit ≠ large**

— **Est-ce que [ce pull] vous plaît?**
— **Oui, il me plaît.**   **Non, il ne me plaît pas.**
   Il est | **joli**   **Il est** | **moche**
   | **super** | **affreux**
   | **élégant** | **ridicule**
   | **bon marché** | **cher**
   | **en solde** | **trop cher**

— **Vous avez choisi?**
— **Oui, je vais acheter [cette robe].**
   Non, | **je ne suis pas décidé(e).**
   | **je vais réfléchir.**
   | **je vais chercher quelque chose**
   | **d'autre.**

Source: NEW ART to illustrate vocabulary in Student Text, p. 351.

References and Activities in the
Extended Teacher's Edition:
a) Lesson 25, p. T351   b) Lesson 28, p. T376

Visual 57 can be used to practice comparisons., e.g.:

Est-ce que la veste bleue est plus grande ou moins grande que la veste rouge?

MEETING NATIONAL STANDARDS

GOAL 1:
COMMUNICATION

STANDARD 1.1
Interpersonal Communication: Engaging in conversation

Have pairs of students imagine conversations between two people in the visual.

Avec un(e) camarade, composez un dialogue entre deux personnes sur le dessin.

MEETING NATIONAL STANDARDS

GOAL 1:
COMMUNICATION

STANDARD 1.3
Presentational Communication: Expression opinions

Have students pick one of the people in the visual, and imagine what that person is thinking about the clothes he/she is trying on, and what others would say if he/she were to wear them to a party.

Choisissez une des personnes du dessin. Imaginez ce qu'il/elle pense des vêtements qu'il/elle essaie et ce que d'autres personnes diraient (would say) *s'il/si elle les portait à une boum.*

DESCRIPTION

Four pairs of items to compare:

Pour chaque illustration, indiquez votre préférence et comparez les deux objets en utilisant les adjectifs suggérés:

- **Préfères-tu la maison blanche ou la maison jaune?**
  **grand/confortable/joli/moderne/intéressant
  [Je préfères la maison blanche. Elle est plus moderne ...]**

- **Préfères-tu la Corvette ou la Mercedes?**
  **confortable/rapide/grand/joli/cher/
  économique**

- **Préfères-tu le chien blanc ou le chien noir?**
  grand/joli/méchant/mignon

- **Préfères-tu la veste de cuir ou le blazer?**
  élégant/léger/confortable/pratique/cher

Source: Illustrations from Activité 4, Student Text, p. 366.

*References and Activities in the
Extended Teacher's Edition:*
a) Lesson 27, p. T366

MEETING NATIONAL STANDARDS

GOAL 4:
COMMPARISONS

STANDARD 4.1
Comparing English and French

- Note how English and French make comparisons:

    The green car is **bigger than** the red car.
    La voiture verte est **plus grande que** la voiture rouge.

    The green car is **more expensive than** the red car.
    La voiture verte est **plus chère que** la voiture rouge.

French always uses **plus** + adjective. English sometimes uses **more** + adjective, and sometimes adds **-er** to the adjective.

- Would students in France have trouble knowing which way to make comparisons in English? What guidelines would you give them?

Remarquez comment on forme les comparaisons en anglais et en français.

En français, on utilise toujours plus + *adjectif.*

Est-ce que des élèves français pourraient (could) trouver difficile de former des comparaisons en anglais? Quelles explications pouvez-vous leur donner pour les aider?

[Actually, students will discover that often one can use both forms, but in a general way, most one-syllable adjectives use **-er** *(nicer)* while all adjectives that have 3 or more syllables use **more** *(more elegant)*. Most two-syllable adjectives can be used both ways *(more happy, happier)*.]

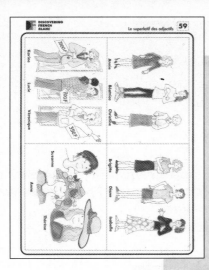

DESCRIPTION

Four sets of drawings to illustrate the use of the superlative.

- **Qui est la fille la plus grande?**
  Béatrice est la fille la plus grande.
  Qui est la fille la plus petite?
  Qui est la fille la plus élégante?

- **Quelle fille porte la jupe la plus longue?**
  C'est Isabelle qui porte la jupe la plus longue.
  Quelle fille porte la jupe la plus courte?
  Quelle fille porte le plus joli pull?

- **Quelle fille porte la veste la plus chère?**
  C'est Karine qui porte la veste la plus chère.
  Quelle fille essaie la veste la moins chère?
  Quelle fille porte la veste la plus chaude?

- **Quelle fille porte le plus petit chapeau?**
  C'est Suzanne qui porte le plus petit chapeau.
  Quelle fille porte le chapeau le plus élégant?
  Quelle fille porte le chapeau le plus drôle?

Source: NEW ART to illustrate superlative adjectives, Student Text, p. 368.

References and Activities in the Extended Teacher's Edition:
a) Lesson 27, p. T368

MEETING NATIONAL STANDARDS

GOAL 1:
COMMUNICATION

STANDARD 1.1
Interpersonal Communication:
Engaging in conversation

Have students act out conversations between the three people in each of the four scenes.

Avec un(e) camarade, composez un dialogue entre trois personnes sur le dessin.

MEETING NATIONAL STANDARDS

GOAL 1:
COMMUNICATION

STANDARD 1.3
Presentational Communication:
Presenting ideas: role-play

Have students pick one of the people in the visual, and imagine that the person is thinking aloud. What would she be saying?

Choisissez une des personnes du dessin, et imaginez qu'il/elle pense tout haut. Qu'est-ce qu'il/elle dit?

DESCRIPTION

Four illustrations showing summer vacation activities.

Où vas-tu aller pendant les vacances?

- **Je vais à la mer.**
  Nous allons louer une villa.

- **Je vais à la montagne.**
  Nous allons rester à l'hôtel.
  [à l'Hôtel Bellevue]

- **Je vais à la campagne.**
  Je vais loger chez des amis.

- **Je vais faire du camping.**
  Marie et sa famille vont louer une caravane.

Combien de temps est-ce que tu vas rester là-bas?
  Je vais passer quinze jours/
  trois semaines/deux mois.

Source: NEW ART to illustrate vocabulary, Student Text, p. 404.

References and Activities in the Extended Teacher's Edition:
a) Lesson 29, p. T404

REVIEW AND PRACTICE

Review the passé composé and the imperfect by asking students to describe the scenes as if they occurred in the past.

Décrivez ces scènes au passé.

MEETING NATIONAL STANDARDS

GOAL 1:
COMMUNICATION

STANDARD 1.1
Interpersonal Communication:
Engaging in conversation

Have pairs of students imagine
conversations between two people
in one of the pictures.

*Avec un(e) camarade, composez un
dialogue entre deux personnes sur
le dessin.*

MEETING NATIONAL STANDARDS

GOAL 1:
COMMUNICATION

STANDARD 1.3
Presentational Communication:
Making lists

Have students pick one of the scenes in
the visual and make a list of what they
would pack if they were spending a
week at that place.

*Choisissez une de ces quatre scènes: vous
allez passer une semaine là. Faites la liste
de ce que vous allez emporter (pack).*

DESCRIPTION

Drawing of a campsite illustrating the following vocabulary:

un sac à dos   **une poêle**
une tente   **une lampe de poche**
un réchaud   **un sac de couchage**
une casserole   **une couverture**

Additional vocabulary:
une table de pique-nique
un raton-laveur

Source: Adaptation of illustrated vocabulary, Student Text, p. 404

References and Activities in the Extended Teacher's Edition:
a) Lesson 29, p. T404

MEETING NATIONAL STANDARDS

GOAL 1:
COMMUNICATION

STANDARD 1.1
Interpersonal Communication:
Engaging in conversation

Have students imagine a conversation between three people in the visual.

Avec un(e) camarade, composez un dialogue entre trois personnes sur le dessin.

MEETING NATIONAL STANDARDS

GOAL 1:
COMMUNICATION

STANDARD 1.1
Interpersonal Communication:
Discussing opinions

Ask students who would like to go camping for a week, and who would not. According to their responses, divide the class into two groups and have them give reasons for their position.

Est-ce que vous voulez aller camper pendant une semaine?

Maintenant, séparez-vous en deux groupes: les Oui et les Non, et donnez vos raisons.

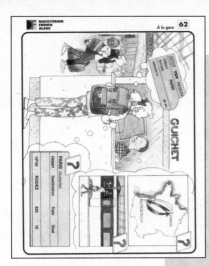

DESCRIPTION

Composite drawing of a French train station to illustrate typical dialogues, such as:

— **Vous désirez, mademoiselle?**
— **Je voudrais un billet de train pour Bordeaux.**
— **Un aller simple?**
— **Non, un aller et retour.**
— **En première classe ou en seconde classe?**
— **En seconde classe, s'il vous plaît.**
— **Voilà, c'est 520 francs.**

— **À quelle heure part le train?**
— **Il part à 15 heures 45.**
— **Et à quelle heure est-ce qu'il arrive à Bordeaux?**
— **Il arrive à 22 heures 10.**

Supplementary vocabulary:
— **De quel quai part le train de Bordeaux?**
— **Il part du quai 5.**

Cultural note:

Regular train service from Paris to Bordeaux leaves from the Gare d'Austerlitz. The trip takes 5 hours or more, depending on the service and number of stops.

The high-speed train (TGV) from Paris to Bordeaux leaves from the Gare Montparnasse. The non-stop TGV makes the trip in three hours.

Source: NEW ART to illustrate vocabulary, Student Text, p. 408.

References and Activities in the Extended Teacher's Edition:
a) Lesson 29, p. T408

REVIEW AND PRACTICE

Review the 24-hour clock which is used in France for official times. Announce afternoon and evening train departures, and have the students convert these times to conversational (American) times, e.g.:

Le train part à 20 heures 50.
Le train part ce soir à huit heures cinquante (à neuf heures moins dix).

MEETING NATIONAL STANDARDS

GOAL 1:
COMMUNICATION

STANDARD 1.1
Interpersonal Communication:
Engaging in conversation

Have pairs of students act out a conversation between a ticket agent and someone who wants to buy a ticket at a French railroad ticket counter.

Avec un(e) camarade, jouez un dialogue entre un(e) employé(e) de gare et une personne qui veut acheter un billet de train.

MEETING NATIONAL STANDARDS

GOAL 1:
COMMUNICATION

STANDARD 1.3
Presentational Communication:
Presenting ideas

Have students pick one of the people in the visual, and imagine that the person is thinking aloud. What would he/she be saying?

Choisissez une des personnes du dessin, et imaginez qu'il/elle pense tout haut. Qu'est-ce qu'il/elle dit?

DESCRIPTION

Eight scenes illustrating the following verbs:

Left-column verbs (with **à**):

- **commencer à** Paul commence à laver sa voiture.
- **apprendre à** Alice apprend à faire du vélo.
- **hésiter à** André hésite à faire la vaisselle.
- **réussir à** Claire réussit à gagner la course.

Right-column verbs (with **de**):

- **essayer de** Marie essaie de réparer sa bicyclette.
- **décider de** Monsieur Masson décide de partir.
- **rêver de** Monique rêve de passer ses vacances en Guadeloupe.
- **oublier de** Roger a oublié de prendre sa raquette.

Source: NEW ART to illustrate vocabulary, Student Text, p. 414.

References and Activities in the Extended Teacher's Edition:
a) Lesson 30, p. T414

MEETING NATIONAL STANDARDS

GOAL 1:
COMMUNICATION

STANDARD 1.3
Presentational Communication: Presenting ideas

Have students pick one of the people in the visual, and imagine that the person is thinking aloud. What would he/she be saying?

Choisissez une des personnes du dessin, et imaginez qu'il/elle pense tout haut. Qu'est-ce qu'il/elle dit?

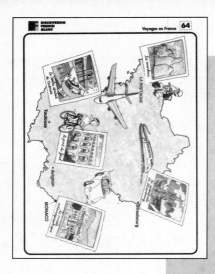

DESCRIPTION

Drawing of five summer travel destinations in France, each showing an important site and illustrating a different mode of transportation. Here are some sample statements using the future tense:

- **Cet été, j'irai en Bretagne.**
  Je voyagerai en scooter.
  Je verrai des menhirs.

- **Cet été, j'irai à Toulouse.**
  Je voyagerai par avion.
  Je visiterai le Centre Spatial.

- **Cet été, j'irai à Strasbourg.**
  Je voyagerai en train.
  Je prendrai des photos de la cathédrale.

- **Cet été, j'irai à Avignon.**
  Je voyagerai à vélo.
  Je me promènerai sur le pont du Gard.

- **Cet été, j'irai à Monaco.**
  Je voyagerai en voiture.
  Je visiterai le Musée océanographique.

Source: NEW ART to illustrate use of future, Student Text, p. 426.

References and Activities in the Extended Teacher's Edition:
a) Lesson 31, p. T426
b) Lesson 31, p. T 423

REVIEW AND PRACTICE

a) Review the passé composé: Have students describe the various trips by using the passé composé.

b) Practice negative forms in the future: Ask questions about the visual which will elicit negative answers.

— **Iras-tu en Espagne cet été?**
— **Non, je n'irai pas en Espagne. J'irai à Avignon.**

MEETING NATIONAL STANDARDS

GOAL 3:
CONNECTIONS

STANDARD 3.2
Using French to find information: Internet

• Have students pick one of the destinations on the visual and use the Internet to find out information about hotels in the area. [http://www.calvacom.fr/relais/accueil.ht]

• Have students use the Internet to find out information about weather in one of the areas in the visual. [http://web.urec.fr/france/france.html]

Choisissez une des destinations montrées et utilisez Internet pour vous renseigner (get information) sur les hôtels de la région. [http://www.calvacom.fr/relais/accueil.ht]

Utilisez Internet pour vous renseigner sur le temps qu'il fait dans une des régions montrées. [http://web.urec.fr/france/france.html]

Note: Website addresses may sometimes change; some addresses may not be accessible, depending on your computer setup.

DESCRIPTION

Two young people are dreaming what they do if...

Olivier: Si j'avais beaucoup d'argent ...
- **je visiterai Paris**
- **j'achèterai une nouvelle voiture/une voiture de sport [une décapotable]**
- **j'irai à l'université aux États-Unis**
- **je donnerai 5000 francs à l'hôpital**

Juliette: Si c'était le mois de juillet ...
- **j'irai à la plage, je jouerai au volley, je ferai de la planche à voile**
- **je ferai du camping, j'observerai des écureuils**
- **je ferai du vélo**
- **j'aurai un job dans un fast-food, je gagnerai de l'argent**

Source: NEW ART to illustrate use of future after **si**, Student Text, p. 425.

References and Activities in the Extended Teacher's Edition:
a) Lesson 31, p. T426
b) Lesson 32, p. 435

a) Practice the negative forms of the future.

> Olivier: *Malheureusement je n'ai pas assez d'argent.*
> *Cette année, je ne visiterai pas Paris.* etc.
>
> Juliette: *Malheureusement, c'est l'hiver.*
> *Ce weekend, je n'irai pas à la plage.* etc.

b) Practice sequence of tenses after **quand.**

> *Quand il aura beaucoup d'argent, Olivier visitera Paris.*
>
> *Quand ce sera le mois de juillet, Juliette ira à la plage.*

MEETING NATIONAL STANDARDS

GOAL 1:
COMMUNICATION

STANDARD 1.3
Presentational Communication: Narrating in the past

Have students imagine that all the wishes expressed in Visual 65 have come true. Write a description of what Olivier or Juliette did.

Tous les souhaits (wishes) *exprimés se sont réalisés* (come true). *Décrivez ce qu'Olivier ou Juliette a fait.*

66 Quelques véhicules

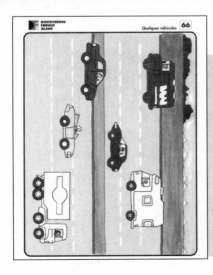

DESCRIPTION

Various types of vehicles on a divided highway.

On peut conduire ...

une camionnette	**une voiture**
une voiture de sport	**une décapotable**
un minivan	**un camion**

Source: Illustrations from Student Text, p. 458

References and Activities in the Extended Teacher's Edition:
a) Lesson 33, p. T458

MEETING NATIONAL STANDARDS

GOAL 1:

COMMUNICATION

STANDARD 1.1

Interpersonal Communication:
Engaging in conversation

Have pairs of students discuss which type of car they would like to have and why.

Avec un(e) camarade, discutez quel genre de voiture vous voudriez avoir, et expliquez pourquoi.

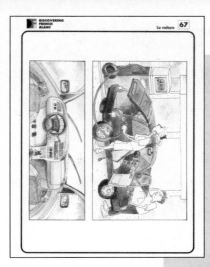

DESCRIPTION

Illustrations showing the parts of a car:

À la station-service:

l'essence	le coffre
un pneu	le réservoir
le toit	le siège
le capot	le clignotant
le moteur	la ceinture de sécurité
le phare	une roue

L'intérieur de la voiture:

le rétroviseur	le klaxon
le pare-brise	la clé
un essuie-glace	le frein
le volant	l'accélérateur

Avant de partir en voyage, il faut...

- faire le plein d'essence
- nettoyer le pare-brise
- vérifier l'huile
- vérifier les freins
- vérifier les pneus

Additional vocabulary:

la pompe à essenceles
feux arrière *(tail lights)*
sans plomb *(lead-free)*
le changement de vitesse *(transmission)*
la pédale de débrayage *(clutch)*

Source: Illustrations from Student Text, p. 460.

References and Activities in the Extended Teacher's Edition:
a) Lesson 33, p. T460

MEETING NATIONAL STANDARDS

GOAL 1:
COMMUNICATION

STANDARD 1.1
Interpersonal Communication:
Engaging in conversation

Imagine that the two people in the visual are getting ready to leave on vacation. Act out the conversation they are having.

Deux personnes sur ce dessin se préparent à partir en vacances. Avec un(e) camarade, imaginez un dialogue approprié.

MEETING NATIONAL STANDARDS

GOAL 1:
COMMUNICATION

STANDARD 1.3
Presentational Communication:
Expressing personal ideas

Have students pick one of the people in the visual, and imagine that the person is thinking aloud. What would he/she be saying?

Choisissez une des personnes du dessin, et imaginez qu'il/elle pense tout haut. Qu'est-ce qu'il/elle dit?

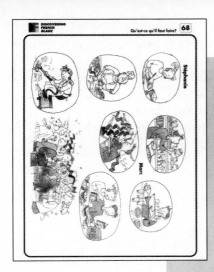

DESCRIPTION

Marc and Stéphanie are planning a party. The drawings in bubbles show how they intend to share in the preparations.

Il faut que Stéphanie... | **écrive/envoie les invitations.**
prépare les sandwiches.
nettoie la maison.

Il faut que Marc... | **achète les boissons.**
mette la table.
décore le salon.

Il faut que Stéphanie et Marc...
choisissent la musique.

Source: NEW ART to accompany Lesson 35, regular subjunctive forms and use of subjunctive with **il faut que**, pp. 472-475.

References and Activities in the Extended Teacher's Edition:
a) Lesson 35, p. T475

REVIEW AND PRACTICE

a) Review the vocabulary by having the students first describe the actions in the present tense.

b) Irregular subjunctives: After Lesson 36, students can also generate sentences with irregular forms:

a) *Décrivez ces activités au passé.*

Il faut que Stéphanie fasse les sandwiches.
Il faut que Marc aille au supermarché. Il faut qu'il fasse les courses.

MEETING NATIONAL STANDARDS

GOAL 1:
COMMUNICATION

STANDARD 1.1
Interpersonal Communication:
Engaging in conversation

Have pairs of students imagine conversations between two people at the party.

Avec un(e) camarade, imaginez un dialogue entre deux personnes à la boum.

MEETING NATIONAL STANDARDS

GOAL 1:
COMMUNICATION

STANDARD 1.3
Presentational Communication:
Narrating in the past

Have students pick either Stéphanie or Marc and imagine that they are writing a letter to a friend describing the party they organized last weekend. Be as detailed as possible.

Vous êtes Stéphanie (ou Marc) et vous écrivez à un copain/une copine pour décrire la boum que vous avez organisée le wekend dernier. Donnez beaucoup de détails.

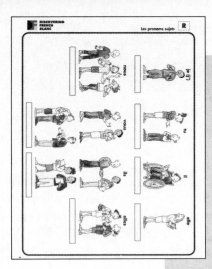

DESCRIPTION

Illustrations of the subject pronouns, with blanks where one can write:

- corresponding verb forms
  (e.g., **suis, es, est**…)
- corresponding object pronouns
  (e.g., **me, te, le**…)
- corresponding stress pronouns
  (e.g., **moi, toi, lui**…)

Source: NEW ART

References and Activities in the Extended Teacher's Edition:
a) Rappel 3, p. T22
b) Rappel 3, p. T23

REVIEW AND PRACTICE

Visual R can be used
- to practice verb forms in rapid drill format
- to review forms of pronouns: subject, direct object, indirect object, stress pronouns, reflexive pronouns

GOAL 4:
COMMUNICATION

STANDARD 4.1
Comparing English and French

(a) Have students observe the similarities and differences between the pronoun systems of French and English in the third person forms.

- In the third person singular, English always distinguishes between male and female (he/she, him/her, to him/to her). What about French?

- In the third person singular, English always distinguishes between persons and objects (he/she *vs.* it). What about French?

- In the third person plural, English does not distinguish between male and female (they). What about French?

- In the third person plural, English does not distinguish between persons and objects (they). What about French?

(b) In the second person, Old English used to distinguish between familiar (thou, thee) and formal (ye). Modern English has only one pronoun (you) which is both familiar and formal, singular and plural.

What about French?

What are the advantages of a language that addresses family and close friends in one way, and other adults and acquaintances in a more formal way? What are the disadvantages?